Praise for

YOUR THOUGHTS CAN CHANGE YOUR LIFE

"This book will actually reach more men and women who are searching for help in solving problems of life than anything I have read in a long time."
— Vernon Howard, author of
Success Through the Magic of Personal Power

"Dr. Curtis has indeed written a fine book, full of rich human interest and experience. It will help many to see their own larger possibilities."
— Dr. Ervin Seale, Church of the Truth,
New York City

"I heartily recommend this book to everyone, whatever his station in life, who wants to live better."
— Dan Custer, author of
The Miracle of Mind Power

DR. DONALD CURTIS is a renowned author, lecturer, and New Thought leader, as well as one of America's best-known and beloved metaphysical teachers.

D0104527

Your Thoughts Can Change Your Life

Donald Curtis

WARNER BOOKS

A Time Warner Company

Warner Books Edition
Copyright © 1974 by Donald Curtis.
Originally published in 1961 by Prentice Hall.

This Warner Book edition is published by arrangement with the author.

Warner Books, Inc., 1271 Avenue of the Americas, New York, NY 10020
Visit our web site at
    http://pathfinder.com/twep

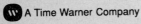 A Time Warner Company

Printed in the United States of America
First Warner Books Printing: August 1996
10 9 8 7 6 5 4 3 2

Library of Congress Cataloging-in-Publication Data

Curtis, Donald.
    Your thoughts can change your life / Donald Curtis.
        p.   cm.
    Originally published: Englewood Cliffs, N.J. : Prentice-Hall,
1961.
    Includes index.
    ISBN 0-446-67196-7
    1. New Thought.   I. Title.
BF639.C885   1996
299'.93—dc20   96-4948
                                                                                            CIP

Cover design by Morris Taub
Cover photo by Jane Vollers

To

Bernice Curtis

1905 – 1995

Table of Contents

Preface to the 1961 Edition

Each individual must make his own adjustment to the problems of the Space Age just as each individual has done through all the ages of history—from the Stone Age through the Atomic Age. The problems facing humanity in the Space Age are no different from the ones in earlier stages of civilization. They are only more so.

This is an age of exploration and expansion. The mysteries of outer space are rapidly being solved. During the lifetime of some of us, we may be able to visit the moon or even a neighboring planet. True, the range of mankind's intellect and experience is expanding at a tremendous rate, but it seems that the farther we are able to reach beyond the earth, the farther we are becoming separated from ourselves. It is obvious that the real need for exploration resides in inner, rather than outer space. Something can be done about this—if we know how to go about it. This book is about how to explore the inner space of your own consciousness.

Preface to the 1996 Edition

During the thirty-five years since *Your Thoughts Can Change Your Life* was first published, our world has continued on an outward trajectory of scientific advance toward knowledge and technical development.

The Space Age has become the Cyber-Space Age, and the Internet and On-Line technologies are opening new windows of communication and discovery in every field of human endeavor throughout the world. Weare proving that we have "dominion over the heavens and the earth."

However, in spite of our conquest of outer space, we still know very little about the inner spaces of our own mental and spiritual consciousness. In the 1961 Preface it says, "It is obvious that the real need for exploration resides in inner rather than outer space." Nothing has changed.

DONALD CURTIS

Your
Thoughts
Can Change
Your Life

1

❖ ❖ ❖

Where Do We Go from Here?

"There's no use taking him upstairs, Joe. He won't last until morning anyway."

Dimly these words soaked into my troubled mind as I struggled to regain consciousness. I was lying on a stretcher in the receiving ward of a large New York hospital one bleak midnight not too many years ago.

My eyes blinked weakly under the merciless glare of the lone overhead light. It was the sound of my own groans that pulled me back to the threshold of awareness; I began to realize that I was still alive. The wracking pain along my right side confirmed that. I writhed helplessly in the grip of the worst suffering I had ever known.

My gasps of agony brought the two white-uniformed interns over to my stretcher. As they gazed down at me, one of them said sardonically. "Well what do you know? He's still with us Joe. Where there's life there's pain, eh? Joe, hand me that needle will you? Might as well make him comfortable for as long as he's around. But as I said, he probably won't make it to morning."

Suddenly I realized, *"He's talking about me!"*

"Hey, wait a minute," I protested. "I'm not ready to die! What are you talking about? This is nothing—I've had this pain all my life. I'll be over it in a couple of days. It's just—"

My voice trailed off as the hypo took hold. I hovered on the brink of consciousness for a few minutes as my life passed in review with terrifying clarity. I realized that this was it. I had come to the end of the road. I was about to die. Actually, the prospect was not too unwelcome. I was too sick to be frightened, and at least it would bring an end to the pain—pain that had plagued me since I was a child.

"At least I won't have to put up with you anymore," I laughed as I struggled with my old antagonist. But even as I said it I knew that it was all an act. I knew that dying would make absolutely no difference. My pain would go with me, because in my delirium I had confirmed what I had always suspected: *My pain was not only in my body. It was in every part of me. I had brought it on and I alone could get rid of it.*

Then and there, I decided I had too much unfinished business to be taken care of! This was no time to die!

By extending all my will power and strength, I called the intern and managed to gasp out the name of a friend who I knew would help me. He could get my own doctor and do whatever else was necessary.

The intern agreed to call my friend. "O.K., Mac," he said. "I'll call him—not that I think it will do much good, but you're the doctor."

Little did he realize—nor did I—the truth he had spoken.

Oh, I had other doctors—a whole crew of them—specialists, surgeons, around-the-clock nurses. But in the final analysis I *was* the doctor.

During the crisis—and after I had come through it successfully—I knew that I had had the help of *something greater* than either myself or the doctors and nurses who had pulled me through. I also discovered a lot of other things. First, I knew that I alone was responsible for my illness. Second, I concluded that by changing what was wrong with me in my character—my inner consciousness—I could get well. Third, I determined to lead an entirely different kind of life when I did get well.

When I was finally released from the hospital for a long period of convalescence, I knew that I had plenty of work to do for the rest of my life. First, however, I had to pick up the threads of my life and my career. A few months before, I had been financially well off, for there were substantial funds in the bank, which I had saved over a number of years as a Hollywood actor. But now those savings were gone and I was deeply in debt. But this didn't really bother me. The important thing was that I was alive! It was getting started on the way back that was my immediate concern.

I sought spiritual guidance—and found it—from Dr. Raymond Charles Barker, minister of the First Church of Religious Science, of New York and from Dr. Ervin Seale, minister of the Church of Truth. These fine men had developed large churches in New York City by teaching the spiritual philosophy of the Science of Mind. This philosophy was successfully rebuilding the lives of thousands of men and women like myself who were seeking help in meeting their problems.

I had previously been exposed to this philosophy in Los Angeles by hearing Dr. Ernest Holmes, the founder of Religious Science. I hadn't followed through on it, however. It took the sledge-hammer blow of my illness to bring me to my senses. I determined to learn more about the Science of Mind teachings so that I could get my life back in order and continue my career as an actor. But as I shuttled back and forth between New York and Hollywood during the next few years, I made little headway in this study, less in my career, and seemingly none at all in my life in general.

I had lost fortune, family (through divorce), and friends. In time, I landed in the hospital again; my body was unable to stand up under the physical, mental and emotional punishment I had given it.

We are not punished for our sins; we are punished by them, I thought as I lay on the operating table. This is a truth that I have never forgotten.

At last I made up my mind that I wasn't going to put off doing what I had to do any longer. I called Dr. Barker and asked for some instruction and prayer treatment while I was in the hospital. He set me straight on a lot of things, and my recovery was rapid and complete.

With Dr. Barker's help, I was healed of something which had been "bugging" me all my life—something in the vast inner space of my psyche—and I have never been ill since, in any but the most minor way.

As soon as I could, I enrolled in all of Dr. Barker's and Dr. Seale's classes. These started me on a road which has led steadily upward to this day, even though there have been many setbacks along the way.

In this book, I shall tell you something of my experiences along that upward road. This book also points out the methods that I have found essential in reconditioning the inner mind—strengthening it so that we can make it a useful servant rather than a destructive master.

Later in this book I will tell you of some of the events which guided me into the teaching of this philosophy and the use of it to help others. But of greater interest here is the teaching itself—the techniques which help people *help themselves* to find meaning in the adventure of life.

Over the years, in addition to teaching and lecturing to large audiences both in person and over radio and television, I have spent the major part of my time working with people on the individual level. I have tried to help them achieve that *inner* change which inevitably leads to improved *outer* conditions in their lives.

A typical case among the thousands whom I have helped is that of a young couple who came to see me a few years ago in New York.

The young woman's crying stopped just long enough for her to sob out, "I don't know what we are going to do, Dr. Curtis. We've tried everything, but we're just not getting anywhere."

I spoke reassuringly, and put out my hand to comfort her. Then the girl's handsome young husband stopped pacing and put his arm around his wife, murmuring, "Now don't cry, honey. That won't help any."

"If we only knew how to pray," she continued. "There must be some way out of this. I know God can help us, but I don't know where to start. We've tried to pray, but I guess we don't know how. At least our kind of prayer isn't getting us anywhere."

There it was again—the frustration of not being able to make any progress against a seemingly hopeless situation. Not an uncommon feeling for any of us, is it? This couple had prayed, but had received no answer. The goal was ahead but they couldn't seem to reach it.

Why? They were simply too bogged down in their problem to help themselves through prayer or any other means. And they were in a mess.

These young people had come to me, as troubled people do every day, because they had not been able to find help anywhere else. Orthodox religion and orthodox psychiatry both have their place in the scheme of things but by themselves they have both proved inadequate in helping people where they most need it—*where they live*—right here and right now.

Understanding, love, and a feeling of identification—these are always necessary qualities for one who would be really helpful. This young couple came to me because I spoke their language. I had been there. Such understanding, plus the development of the techniques described in this book, have helped me help others, even though I may not always be able to help myself.

Moreover, everytime someone else is helped by the application of the scientific principles of right thinking, I—and all of us—are also helped. This is the great work of this modern age: to combat the forces of darkness with forces of light, thereby dissolving the negative and destructive tendencies within the individual and the race so that we may attain a higher level of experience. And the level of society as a whole cannot help but be raised as the individual conquers his problems through inner change.

Part of my techniques of teaching is to remember my own experiences in solving problems, then to apply spiritual principles to helping others solve theirs. I often establish a bond of confidence by saying, "Come on now, relax and tell me all about it. There is nothing you can say which can surprise me. I have done just about everything wrong at least once—some things many times. I'm no great shakes as an example, but I can show you how, with the help of the great principle of right action, you can help yourself." This always works, just as it did with our young couple.

Briefly, that young couple's situation was this: Against parental opposition, they had married while still in their teens. The husband was singing on a television program in New York. For a few months, their lives were filled with love, success and gaiety. But they awoke one morning to find that the television program had been cancelled. The girl bride was expecting, and youthful improvidence had left them in no financial circumstances to meet either situation.

Still, they weren't too worried. The illusion of "easy come, easy go" was still fresh in their minds. Something would turn up!

"Why, honey," the young bride exclaimed, "You're the greatest singer in the world! Everyone will be wanting you to sing on their programs. You just wait and see. And as for our baby, I'm so excited I can hardly wait! There's nothing to worry about, darling. Women have babies every day."

They lived on love and laughter for a time, but finally the grim realities of existence became increasingly clear. The young man might have been the greatest singer in the world, but Broadway and TV somehow remained unaware of it. The few minor singing jobs he could get were insufficient to meet expenses. Finally, after moving to a series of cheaper apartments, they were evicted for non-payment of rent with only days to go before the baby was due.

I listened to this story as it tumbled out of both youngsters. It was now two years later, the baby had been born, and they had managed somehow. They young parents would soon be twenty-one, just about the time their daughter would celebrate her second birthday. Moreover, their second child was on the way. The young man's singing career had never gotten off the ground, and they had lived from hand to mouth with only an occasional job to sustain them. The couple's parents had relented and forgiven long enough to help them with expenses for the delivery of the first baby, but now this help had been cut off when the couple refused to give up the dreams of a career in the big city and to return to the security of the boy's father's business in a small New England town.

Moreover, there had been a lack of proper food which had caused illness in the little family. The youngster was obviously suffering from malnutrition, as I am sure the mother was also.

They had tried everything, including prayer, and had finally come to me as a sort of last resort. I was able to help them by making them help themselves. I made clear to them that *the nature of our lives is determined by the nature of our inner attitudes and mind.*

We know intuitively that we can live and think and pray in such a way that we can move from where we are to where we want to be. This young couple finally understood this. They also knew, as all of us do, that this "way" is something that each of us must develop for himself.

No one can solve our problems for us. No one can grow for us.

But there is always help and guidance for those who seek it and are willing to follow through in applying sound spiritual and mental principles to this business of living.

My young friends were eager students indeed. By being willing to help themselves, they were not only able to solve their current problems, but they developed an approach to life which, if it didn't exactly move them along to where they thought they wanted to be, did result in getting them out of their immediate difficulties.

The lives of this young couple began to change because *when we change our inner thoughts, feelings and attitudes, our outer experiences will change automatically. There is a definite relationship between what goes on inside of us and what happens in our world. This understanding is the beginning of wisdom and harmonious, purposeful living.*

Today several million people in this country alone are also changing their lives for the better by applying simple spiritual, mental and emotional disciplines to the everyday situations of life. Constructive attention to these three inner levels builds an inner equivalent of what we want to do, have and experience. Remember: nothing can happen on the outside until it happens first on the inside.

In starting the young couple on the path upward, I worked with them on twelve basic constructive mental attitudes which changed their lives. These same twelve steps have not only transformed my own life, but have led the way to more abundant living for the many with whom I have personally counseled.

These steps progress toward integrating our whole being. They develop our understanding to the point where we are capable of entertaining larger ideas, thereby bringing us larger patterns of experience. They are a ground plan for living. Their range includes thought, prayer and action.

In this book we are not concerned with a lengthy analysis of negative mental and emotional factors of causation. This material is well-covered in many other excellent books. Here we intend to develop these twelve attitudes—attitudes that will give us the inner strength and resourcefulness to meet the challenges of everyday living.

Here are the twelve steps:

1. Relaxation
2. Expectation
3. Recognition
4. Unification
5. Dedication
6. Intention
7. Identification
8. Conviction
9. Realization
10. Projection
11. Action
12. Cooperation

Suggestions for Personal Use

1. Study each step as explained in the following chapters and meditate upon it as part of a ground plan for your life.
2. Start right here—right now—applying these 12 steps to your life in general.
3. Apply the 12 steps to any particular condition, problem or situation that may confront you.
4. Go through the steps whenever you are faced with any problem or situation to which you want to bring your fullest power and ability.
5. Start the day by going through this sequence of steps as soon as possible upon arising. Repeat it before retiring.

As we strengthen our inner power by developing our understanding and use of these steps, we move inevitably into the conquest of "inner space," the area out of which come the issues of life.

We are all living in the space age. Let's learn—right now—how to go into orbit.

2

❖ ❖ ❖

The Art of Sitting Loose

"Places, please. Places!" The stage manager knocked at the door of my dressing room as the curtain was about to go up on the opening night of another play.

How I had looked forward to it! My part was a fine one, and the weeks of rehearsal had been sheer pleasure. But now that it was opening night, again there was pain—wracking, disintegrating pain. My hands shook, perspiration stood out on my forehead as I struggled to complete my makeup. At the same time I was trying to hold a hot water bottle against my bare back as a counter-irritant to the pain.

"Please, God, just let me get on stage," I implored. "Then I know I'll be all right."

Years ago I had discovered that once I got into the play and was acting with sufficient intensity, the pain would disappear. It was only years later that I realized the principle involved. *As soon as I took my mind off the pain and put it on the business at hand, the pain disappeared.*

But where did the pain come from in the first place? Did it indicate a functional or an organic disorder? No one, including medical specialists, could explain why I should experience this periodic shattering pain—*a pain that always appeared just before I had anything important to do.*

After everything failed, my old family doctor simply said, "I guess you'll just have to live with it, son. Maybe you'll grow out of it."

Unwittingly, he had touched the key to the problem! *I did need to grow out of it.* And not physically, either. I needed to grow out of the inner attitudes of fear, nervousness, tension and pressure which were aggravating an already existing bodily weakness. At the time, however, I was not aware of how to do this. Thus the wear and tear on my body continued—inevitably culminating in the incident with which I opened this book.

It took this extreme experience to show me the relationship between my mental and emotional attitudes and the condition of my body. That this relationship is real had been thoroughly proved during the past several years, but the majority of people still do not relate the state of their minds to the conditions of their experience. That is why this book was written—to help develop those attitudes and states of consciousness which will free the natural inner forces that make for health, happiness, abundance, and freedom in our lives.

Remember, however, that I was not healed of my condition until I changed my *inner* state of mind. The effects will not disappear until the cause is removed. True, the surgeon removed a part of my body which saved my life and stopped the pain—but only temporarily. The doctor can save the life, but it can only continue to be saved if the inner consciousness is cooperating with the natural forces of life which flow through us all. Tension, pressure and anxiety block this flow. When we are tense we become tired, nervous, irritable and eventually ill. When we resist the natural harmony, balance and flow of life forces, something has to give—usually in our bodies. But remember: the body is acted upon by the mind. Disordered thinking and imbalanced emotional adjustment are what produce disorders in our bodies.

It is generally agreed that *relaxation* is the starting point for harmonious living. Tension is undoubtedly the greatest single cause of trouble and unhappiness. It can express itself in many ways and can be caused by many things. But it has only one cure—relaxation.

There is absolutely no limit to the healing power of the great forces of life within us if we learn to relax, cooperate, and let relief come.

For example, I once lost my voice just before the opening of a play. Sprays, gargles and poultices were of no help whatsoever. How could they be? These were merely surface remedies. *Healing can only be accomplished by treating the cause underlying the illness.* Naturally, tension, nervousness and worry over the opening of the play had caused my laryngitis.

At last, through the help of a spiritual mind practitioner I relaxed sufficiently to be able to speak by curtain time. As soon as I was on stage all destructive tension left me. I became relaxed, my voice cleared up completely. The principle again: *When our inner adjustment is balanced and relaxed, our external experience and action will be the same.*

An elderly woman once expressed to me her philosophy of relaxation as follows: "When I run, I walk, and when I sit I sit loose. And when I worry, I go to sleep."

This woman let nothing disturb her in any way. She was relaxed. Intuitively she realized that relaxation is power and that all good things proceed from the quiet mind.

An ancient Chinese proverb says, "He who conquers a city is great. He who conquers himself is mighty." A person who learns to relax mentally, emotionally and physically is on the road to accomplishment because he has conquered himself.

All too often, however, we are like the confused cowboy who mounted up and "rode off in all directions at once." Unless we learn to run things from a relaxed center within ourselves, we are going to be run by anything and everything that comes along.

Recently a well-known television executive dashed into his office, highly excited. Scattering papers and assistants like leaves in the wind, he shouted for his secretary to start making some telephone calls.

"Whom shall I call, sir?" she inquired timidly.

"Don't bother me with details," he shouted. "What difference does it make? Call anybody! Don't just stand there! Get on the phone! We're wasting time."

Like Martha in the Bible, he was "troubled about many things."

Caught up in a pressure situation of his own making, he had neither the inclination nor the ability to stop it. Relaxation and he were complete strangers, yet here was a man who was directly responsible for sending out several hours of TV entertainment to the nation each week—programs gauged for enjoyment and relaxation!

Not too long ago I gave a friend of mine—an important Hollywood producer—Dr. David Fink's book called *For People Under Pressure*.* I wish he had read it. If he had, he might still be alive today. As I left his office I heard him say to his secretary, "Miss Smith, please type me a report covering the high points of this book, will you? I'm under too much pressure to read it."

Unfortunately, this man recently joined the ranks of those who have fallen "in harness"—not so much from overwork as from an inability to relax.

In direct contrast to these members of the "suicide squadron" are those low-pressure types who enjoy twice the success with half the trouble.

Bing Crosby was one of them. He learned the value of relaxation. His inner calm was contagious. It made us feel good just to watch him. For this reason, the romance between Bing and the world grew mutually as the years rolled on.

Many years ago, when I was beginning as a radio actor in Hollywood, I was called for a small part on a show on which Bing Crosby was the guest star. He was his usual relaxed self right up to air time. The rest of us, however, all felt the mounting tension as we waited for the producer to give the signal that we were on the air.

The producer raised his arm for the signal. Then with only ten seconds to go, Bing dropped his script. Panic broke loose—in everyone but Bing. While actors, agency men, stage hands and musicians scrambled to pick up the fluttering pages of the script, Bing nonchalantly bent down, picked up the elusive first page, cocked his hat on the back of his head, and came in exactly on cue. That night he gave a tremendous performance without any fuss whatsoever.

Bing's performances looked easy. So did those of Jimmy Stewart another "relaxation specialist." These two gentlemen learned to "sit

* Simon and Schuster, New York, 1956

loose." They stayed quiet and calm on the inside and let the outside take care of itself.

You may say, "Oh, that came naturally to *them*. I could relax too if I 'had it made' the way those two did. They didn't have the worries I have."

Don't you believe it. Jimmy Stewart and Bing Crosby both had to learn how to relax themselves. If you doubt it, take a look at some of their early efforts before the motion picture cameras. Indeed, I am sure that they were able to make a success of their careers simply because they forced themselves to master the art of relaxation.

There is also a story about a Hollywood "western" hero of an earlier day that points up the need for a relaxed approach to life. This particular actor was making one of a long series of "quickies" in which all corners were cut to save time and money during production. Shooting schedules were crowded and cowboys and Indians were acting steadily from sunup until past midnight.

In the middle of one scene, our hero finally rebelled. For weeks he had been before the cameras twelve to fourteen hours a day. He was hungry and ready to drop, but still the director was prodding him to work even harder.

Then, in a burst of irrefutable logic, the actor exclaimed, "Wait a minute, who's in such a hurry to see this picture anyway?"

When we are caught up in daily pressures, we might well ask ourselves some similar questions: "Who *is* in such a hurry besides me? Is this matter really so urgent or am I just making it that way? Is this project really important or am I kidding myself? Am I really under pressure or do I just have the pressure habit? What would happen if I just forgot everything and went fishing?"

Try asking these questions sometime. Honest answers will help you relax and break the pressure habit.

Here is the point. Successful, popular and prosperous people have not become so because of outer circumstances, luck, "the breaks," or anything similar. They—and we too—enjoy success when real inner confidence is developed. We have harmony in our personal relationships when we really love life and people. *We experience order and ease in our lives when we relax inside and learn to "let go and let God."*

Be Willing to Change

For every outer effect there is a corresponding inner cause. Refute and reject this principle though we will, it constantly functions throughout all of life. On the human level it is a matter of understanding that what we experience corresponds directly to what we are.

This is sometimes difficult to accept, but even though the human ego may reject the idea, the real self intuitively knows that it is true. So it becomes a question of, "What are we going to do about it?"

One answer is to keep going just the way we are, resisting change and growth, buffeted about by the complexities of modern civilization—tense, tired and terrified. Or—we can take a stand.

And taking that stand means simply this: *if we want to change our world we must first change ourselves.* Most of us can stand considerable mental and emotional re-tooling; we should not be too stubborn or proud to admit it and do something about it.

Relaxation is the starting point.

What Is Relaxation?

Very simply, relaxation is the ability to "sit loose." It is perhaps that hypothetical perfect state of existence where all of our parts and functions are in perfect order. It is the integrated balance between our spiritual, mental and physical natures that results in harmonious relationship with God, ourselves and our world.

Relaxation means releasing all concern and tension and letting the natural order of life flow through one's whole being. Relaxation is "doing what comes naturally." Relaxation is the result of "letting go and letting God."

Relaxation is also the realization that even though we may not know what lies ahead, we are confident that it can only be good. Moreover, relaxation is the realization that since we will probably never get all the things done that we want to do, it is better to approach life easily and realistically, doing the best we can, and not being too demanding of ourselves.

Now let's go ahead and find out how we can best achieve relaxation.

Why We Should Relax

Getting started in anything worthwhile is never easy. Solid accomplishment can only come as the result of thorough preparation, sincere dedication, and constant application to the business at hand. My own experience is a case in point. When I first came to Hollywood a number of years ago, I was tense. I also had a lot to learn about acting; however, nothing could persuade me that I was anything less than God's gift to the motion picture industry. Accordingly, I had abandoned a promising educational career after having been one of the youngest members of the American Association of University Professors, plus a recipient of a Rockefeller Foundation Fellowship.

By dint of tremendous effort and will-power which all but obscured whatever talent I had, I managed to enjoy considerable success in motion pictures, on the New York stage, and on radio and television. This success continued for a number of years. However, as far as my own ambition and sense of values were concerned, I was always missing the boat.

Why? Because I had never learned to relax, either in life or during a theatrical performance. I was always trying too hard, overselling, pressing, putting *both* best feet forward at the same time.

Nevertheless, at the time I started in Hollywood, I seemed to enjoy a successful career. For a time I couldn't seem to do anything wrong. All the magic doors opened at once. I had my choice of motion picture and radio assignments. Naturally, I saw no reason to diminish my good opinion of myself.

But then, as the old silent movie captions used to say, "came the dawn." The motion picture cameras were not fooled by my outer display of confidence. They saw me as I really was inside—over-eager, insecure, desperate and uncertain.

What was I trying to prove? *That I could do the things I was afraid I couldn't do.* Naturally, I began to fail. Then I hit the bottom—several times.

As soon as the cameras and microphones exposed my inner tensions, the movie producers dropped me like a hot potato. I sank into that frustrated mass of Hollywood humanity which lives in the limbo of bit parts and occasional assignments.

It had been several months between jobs. I just couldn't get back inside the studio gates. My family was regularly subsisting on carrots and hamburger. Then one day it came—that call for which I had been waiting by the telephone for months.

My agent had lined up an interview for a part in a picture. It was a small studio and a minor role in a "B" picture, but it was acting. Here was a chance to get started again.

My heart was pounding as I dressed in my one remaining good suit and met my agent at the producer's office. I had to have that job! I got myself well in hand, exuding confidence, ease, and ability. I had already talked myself into an engagement, but then the dam burst. Instead of obeying the time-honored actors' dictum, "Get set and get out," I got caught up in my own inner pressures and anxieties. I kept talking, telling the producer what a good actor I was, what a fine job I would do in his picture. When I started he had confidence in me. But when I had finished, he certainly had none. I had talked myself in and out of a job in less than five minutes!

Nevertheless, I later realized that it was a right and necessary thing to have happened. The job would have paid me a few hundred dollars, but the experience has been worth a million to me. It taught me one practical truth: *relaxation is good business.*

Any successful business man knows this. Customers are attracted to a harmonious atmosphere, and are much more likely to buy when the atmosphere is relaxed. The merchant, tradesman and professional man alike all profit from cultivating an inner feeling of relaxation. It helps to create a similar atmosphere in everything around you.

When pressures are released, all that is best in us has a chance to take over. Ill-temper, irritation and anxiety all disappear when we are relaxed. Good humor is the natural result, and this is one of the greatest business assets in the world.

In a sense, everyone is in business. We can only succeed outside if we are right inside. This means that we must start with relaxation. Pressure kills prosperity; relaxation builds it.

Here is precisely why relaxation is good business:

1. Relaxation Quiets the Mind

We can think of only one thing at a time, but unless we are asleep, we are always thinking of *something*. This is what gets us into trouble, but at the same time it is also what gets us out! The trick is in learning to control what we are thinking about. When we control our thought, we control our world. If our thoughts control us, the world controls us, and we are at the mercy of every situation and experience that comes along.

The brain is like a giant collection of billions of photoelectric cells, flashing on and off as they are called into use by our thoughts and ideas. When we are scatterbrained and disconnected in our thinking, the overactivity and confused flashing of the lights generate heat and pressure; we become tense and irritable. Headaches, nervousness and various kinds of congestion may result.

But when we learn to think in a straight line with judgment and purpose, the brain center involved begins to glow steadily. Gradually it lights up the cells around it until the entire brain and nervous system is cooperating in accomplishing the business at hand.

In learning to relax, we are engaged in an activity of "self-emptying and God-filling." We simply rid the mind of all the things that don't belong there and focus it upon unlimited ideas and larger concepts. This quiets the mind so that it becomes a channel through which the inner creative power may flow.

2. Relaxation Rebuilds the Body

The constant stream of thought which flows through our minds must go somewhere and become something. The first area of materialization is our own body. The formation of our bodies up to the time of birth was completely taken care of by a power that operated independently of our conscious thought, for at this time we had no conscious thought. Our opportunity to cooperate with this creating, sustaining, and maintaining power came after birth; it continues throughout our lives. Everything we think and feel conditions what happens to the natural full action of life that continues to flow through us.

If we interfere with this action by allowing negative and destructive attitudes and thoughts to fill our minds, our bodies will show the results. Remember: *disease results from destructive mental and emotional attitudes.* In the early stages disease shows up as congestion, pain, fatigue and weaknesses of various kinds. Allowed to continue uncorrected, this negative use of the life force gradually wears down and destroys the body.

Remember, however, that the thing that makes you sick also makes you well. As we learn to cooperate with the life force within us, it corrects negative conditions and rebuilds the body along the lines of the original specifications. This cooperation is our participation in the continuous action of an indwelling healing presence whose functioning is constant.

3. Relaxation Can "Put Humpty-Dumpty Together Again"

Modern science confirms that there are unknown levels in man which must be taken into consideration when working toward our goal of integrating the "whole man." Modern medicine is recognizing that the body cannot be treated as a thing apart, but that consideration must be given to mental, emotional and spiritual factors if the individual is to be "made whole."

Today's forward-looking physicians make provisions for patients to undergo psychological and spiritual therapy at the same time that the physical condition is treated. Indeed, in a number of instances this is accomplished under the same roof. Practitioners on every level now realize that effective treatment and therapy for any condition cannot be concerned merely with the condition alone. It must also work at the point of cause, removing negative mental and emotional attitudes and establishing those of a more constructive nature.

No one engages in negative and destructive thoughts and feelings because they want to. They are the result of immaturity and ignorance. As people grow mentally and spiritually, however, they see the need for change; but by that time their minds have become so conditioned by old habit patterns that they find it next to impossible to change them. The harder they try the less headway they make.

The more they fight their lower natures the stronger they get. This is obviously not the way to change. We cannot conquer a problem or a fault by fighting it; we must dissolve it.

How can we do this? Jesus said, "Resist not evil," but overcome evil with good. Here is the key to relaxation and the key to growth. This maxim also explains why we cannot change ourselves by our mental efforts alone. If we want to change conditions, we must be willing to change ourselves. To develop we must grow, and to grow we must change. An ulcer won't disappear as long as the patient continues to nurse a burning resentment. This cause-and-effect relationship always exists between our experience and our mental attitudes.

4. Relaxation is the First Step in Change for the Better

When we "sit loose" all over—mentally, emotionally and physically—we will be letting go of purely personal concerns and will be giving an integrating force a chance to start working through us. This integration is the real goal we are working toward. It won't be complete, of course, until we develop our basic twelve steps—but relaxation is the place to start.

5. Relaxation Comes from Understanding Yourself

Now what do we do about learning to relax? Right at this point we start by learning to understand a bit more about ourselves. As we grow by the use of our twelve Guides to Life, we will grow automatically; we can't help it. It is our nature to grow.

We are interested in developing those parts of ourselves which we can do something about; namely the mind, the emotions and the body. When we develop and integrate these three areas, we will attain worthwhile and permanent growth.

Look at it this way: the only thing we can really change is our minds. This is done by focusing upon new thoughts and ideas. When the mind is changed, everything else changes. Paul says, "Be ye transformed by the renewing of your mind."

This knowledge alone relaxes us because it shows us that we each hold our fate in our own hands. The law of averages, luck, chance and superstition are all transcended when we grasp the principle of mental causation.

When the mind is turned toward good and stays turned in that direction, all good things follow as a matter of course.

A PROGRAM FOR GENERAL RELAXATION

The importance of a relaxed way of life cannot be stressed too highly. General relaxation can be attained in various ways, and every one of us has our own way of "taking our mind off things." Specific techniques of relaxation on the mental, emotional and physical levels will be taken up later, but if we learn that one of the basic laws of life is "Easy does it," we will never need them.

The following general suggestions will bring relaxation on every level. Together they will produce a balanced life.

1. Adequate rest and sleep.
2. Regular exercise (including all sports and walking).
3. Sensible personal hygiene and bodily care.
   a Baths and showers.
   b. Grooming.
   c. Massages.
   d. Medical attention.
4. Proper scheduling of daily activities.
5. Pleasurable occupation.
6. Planned recreation (including dancing, shows, movies, games, TV, driving).
7. Joyous family and personal relationships.
   a. Dining.
   b. Conversation.
   c. Working, playing and planning together.
8. Avocations and hobbies.
9. Social and community service.
   a. Interest in government.
   b. Committee service.
   c. Club and organizational activities.
10. Contact with nature.
11. Reasonable amount of travel.
12. Reading.

13. Music.
14. Literary and artistic expression, appreciation or creation.
15. Development of the inner life.
    a. Thought, meditation, prayer.
    b. Church membership and activity.

Reasonable attention to the above program will fill our lives with interesting, purposeful, balanced, and therefore relaxed activity.

How to Attain Physical Relaxation

A good part of becoming relaxed is *simply to relax.* Start this at the physical level by learning to actually and literally "sit loose." The model for complete relaxation is deep sleep, and these simple suggestions will assist us in achieving that at the proper time, but right now we want to work toward habitual relaxation in everything we do.

True physical relaxation, of course, goes hand in hand with mental and emotional relaxation; but each of these levels contributes to the whole, and we can start with any one of them. There are many excellent books on the subject; also, some people have their own pet procedures for relaxing. If these do the job for you, continue to use them.

Personally, I find any one and all of the following aids useful in achieving physical relaxation:

1. Deep breathing.
2. Intensive physical exercise of any kind.
3. Shaking the arms and wrists.
4. Rotating the head and trunk.
5. "Slumping"—removing all postural tensions and letting the body fall in a heap.
6. Standing on the head for brief periods.
7. Lying flat on the floor with legs spread and arms extended.
8. Standing barefooted with as few clothes on as possible, moving or standing still according to impulse.
9. Singing and making loud verbal noises.

10. Sitting perfectly still in the most comfortable position possible, doing nothing and thinking of nothing.

To these could well be added an occasional steam bath and massage or perhaps some good osteopathic or chiropractic adjustments from a reputable practitioner.

UNDERSTANDING EMOTIONAL RELAXATION

We can't feel relaxed without *being* that way, and we can't be that way without *feeling* that way. The two go together. One is cause, the other effect. The way we "feel" about things is the cause of most of our experience. Recently I compiled a list of over one hundred destructive emotional attitudes, any one of which can make relaxation impossible.

Here are some members of my emotional "Jukes family" which are always willing to take up residence whenever we are willing to give them room: irritation, anger, hurt, worry, sorrow, hate, fear, bitterness, resentment, remorse, depression, prejudice, pride, greed, dread.

Any one of these destructive emotional attitudes can weigh us down until a normal, healthy approach to life is impossible. Hate can be a "monkey on the back" just as surely as heroin.

It is only common sense to realize that we must do our own emotional housecleaning ourselves. Modern medicine estimates that at least 70 per cent of all functional diseases can be traced to psychosomatic (mental and emotional) factors. Some physicians have gone so far as to estimate that *all* disease is caused by this inner conflict and imbalance. The importance of doing something about it is obvious.

HOW DO I RID MYSELF OF A DESTRUCTIVE EMOTIONAL ATTITUDE?

Let's take the granddaddy of all these destructive attitudes—fear. It is impossible to relax when we are afraid of things—and we are *all* afraid of something, whether we are consciously aware of it or not.

The one basic fear common to the human race is fear of death. An individual's spiritual development can be largely determined by the progress he has made in overcoming this basic fear. This may well be the chief business of our lives, because our appreciation of life and our capacity to live grows directly in proportion to how much we overcome our fear of death. Paradoxically, this also means overcoming our fear of life.

Fear is the *negative* expression of the basic emotion of which faith is the *constructive* expression. Faith is that emotional attitude which says "yes" to life; it is expressed by love, and all the benevolent feelings and attitudes of which we are capable.

Moreover, the fear family includes all the destructive feelings, attitudes and emotions mentioned above. The faith family, on the other hand, includes their opposites: love, kindness, sweetness, benevolence, consideration, forgiveness, encouragement, generosity.

The way to emotional relaxation and re-education is really very simple: *just change families.* Trade fear for faith, confusion for composure, hate for love, anger for calm, dread for anticipation, depression for elation, and resentment for forgiveness. There is no other way. We can never be completely relaxed or balanced as long as we hang on to our destructive feelings.

We get rid of a destructive emotional attitude by consciously developing the opposite constructive feeling as shown above. This includes two basic steps:

1. Analyze your present undesirable feeling and decide what its opposite constructive attitude is.
2. Use every means at your disposal to develop the good feeling.

Although this sounds simple in theory, it may prove difficult to accomplish in fact. Yet anyone can do it if they want to. Of course, a hateful person isn't likely to change into a loving one overnight just by deciding to do so. The point is—he will never change if he doesn't make the decision. Once made, it is a matter of determination and growth.

A young lady once came to my wife Bernice for counsel and guidance. For some time she had been consistently running a temperature of one or two degrees above normal.

In our work with such individual cases, we encourage the person to express herself freely. In this non-directive approach, the individual often reveals the cause of her problem by revealing herself. We have trained ourselves to put two and two together, and we find that with the help of a few well-placed suggestions, the individual can arrive at the cause of her own problem.

The young lady with the fever was no exception. Her conversation went something like this:

"I just can't seem to get anyplace. I don't like my job, or the people I have to work with. It just burns me up the way the boss treats me. I resent the way he talks to me, but I'm afraid to quit for fear I won't be able to get anything else. And I hate the place where I have to live—a dingy hotel room. It just burns me up that my sister lives in a great big fancy home and I have to stay in a dump like that.

"Sometimes I get so desperate," she went on, "that I don't know what to do. I'd just like to die. I never see anybody any more, and I never have enough energy to do anything. Sure, I'd like to get married, but I just burns me up the way the men are these days. My sister has a wonderful husband and three kids, and she's always asking me to come out and stay with them, but I know she just does it so she can rub it in. She's always done that. She's so high and mighty. She burns me up. Mrs. Curtis, do you have any idea why I have this fever?"

My wife smiled faintly. "Let me ask you the same question—what do you think?"

"Well, I don't know. I had tuberculosis, but that's supposed to be all cleared up. Maybe that's still causing the fever," the girl replied.

There followed a short discussion in which Bernice pointed out that intense feelings of longing, jealousy, suppressed resentment and extreme selfishness could well cause tuberculosis. The young lady listened intently, then flushed as she realized that she herself had revealed all of these negative emotional traits.

She was an intelligent young woman. The shoe fit and she put it on. Then she asked, "But what about the fever?"

Bernice simply asked, "How many times have you said 'That burns me up' in the last five minutes?"

Then the bottled-up torrents rushed forth, as the young lady sobbed, "I've brought it all on myself, haven't I—every bit of it. I thought I was getting even with my sister and everyone else, but I've just been taking it out on myself, haven't I?"

"Yes, dear, you have," Bernice replied. "But there is no need to cry about it. Let's change the situation."

"How?"

"By forgiving."

"Forgiving?"

"Exactly. To forgive means 'to give for.' Instead of the feeling of hate and resentment which you have had for so many people and so many things, we are going to give a feeling of love and good will."

"Oh, I couldn't do that!"

"Let's try. Will you do this for the next week: whenever you feel like saying, 'That burns me up,' says instead, 'I like that.' "

The young lady agreed, and a week later she was in a greatly improved mental and physical condition. During the second week it was suggested that she say, "I *like* that," with emphasis on the "like." The improvement continued and so did the attention on her part. After another week, during which she said, "I *love* that" instead of the old "that burns me up," a physical check-up showed that her temperature was normal; moreover, it remained so permanently, and soon there was a general turn for the better in her life.

This young woman was healed of her problems, and a chronic physical condition, through the relaxing techniques of forgiveness. The emotional cause of her unhappiness was dissolved and the resulting inner relaxation reflected itself in her experience. The same process is available to every one of us.

Relaxation Connects Us with the Inner Source of Wisdom and Power

A friend of mine, an author who was a famous Hollywood writer-director-producer, illustrates the importance of relaxation in his story of how one of his best-selling books came to be written.

Already popular as a writer of children's stories for grown-ups, he had contracted to deliver a book to his publishers at a certain date. But he had difficulty with the story, and as the deadline date approached, the pressure and tension shut him off from his source of inspiration. The more he struggled, the worse the situation became; he just wasn't getting anywhere. After one particularly fruitless day at his typewriter, he disgustedly threw himself, exhausted, upon the sofa in his study, ready to give up the whole thing.

Then he fell into a deep sleep and dreamed that the top of his head was a giant funnel, into which were pouring all of the thoughts and ideas that ever existed. It seemed to him that a great ocean of intelligence was flowing down into this funnel. Suddenly this intelligence started to take the form of a story. It unfolded from beginning to end in the dream—clear, concise, and well-constructed. Awakening refreshed, my friend resumed his work on the book and followed through to its completion, setting down exactly what had come to him in the dream.

Exactly what happened here, and what can we learn from it? It is really very simple. When we relax our personal tensions, we open our minds to the influx of a superior intelligence which tells us what we need to know and accomplishes through us what needs to be done. This great reservoir of wisdom and inspiration is the universal mind of God of which our individual minds are a part. Each one of us can think with this greater mind when we relax our personal minds, clear the channel, and let the power flow through.

One young man who came to me was tied up in several kinds of mental, emotional and physical knots over a personal problem. He despaired of winning out over the seemingly great forces which plagued him, but I listened to his story patiently.

"I just can't seem to win," he burst out in anguish.

"You could," I observed, "if you would just remember one thing."

"What's that?"

"*If you don't fight a thing, you can't lose.*"

That did it. Those few simple words had a marvelous effect upon him. He sat down quietly and listened as I explained to him the healing power of a quiet, relaxed mind. I showed him that instead of fighting the problem he needed to reverse his attitude about it.

"What do you mean?" he asked.

"Start to look at the situation in a different way," I explained. "There are always new aspects of it that you have never thought of. By dwelling upon them you will start to think and feel differently about the whole matter."

This young man told me that he would take my advice and give it a try. A few weeks later I was delighted to see that he was a changed person.

"You were right, doctor," he said. "It worked. Changing the thought changed the whole situation. I'm not fighting the problem now and darned if I'm not *winning!*"

Four Effective Pointers on How to Relax

In addition to the general program for relaxation given previously, the following is a "short course" in relaxation that I have found will work effectively in every situation:

1. Stop thinking about what's bothering you.
2. Get comfortable and think of something pleasant.
3. Visualize energy and good flowing in.
4. Know that this energy is building good things in your life.

Before we go on to the discussion of our next great creative attitude—expectation—take time to assimilate the peace and power in the following meditation. The ideas contained in it will quiet and soothe you, and remove all confusion and tension from your mind, your emotions, and your body. After you have let the meditation relax you, come back to it a little later on, and read it again before you go to sleep at night. Use it again tomorrow to start your day, and periodically whenever tension mounts.

DAILY GUIDE TO RELAXATION

Today I stop all personal effort. I stop trying to make things happen. I release all concern about myself, anything, or anybody. I relax, let go and let God. I float serenely above the affairs of the day, untroubled by people or things. At this moment I think nothing, I feel nothing, I do nothing. I detach myself from the outside of my life and connect myself to the inside.

As I make this inner contact, I simply relax and let whatever happens happen. I know I can't force it, so I simply relax and put myself on the receiving end of all the good which is coming my way. I immerse myself in the warm and friendly waters of the abundant life, and let the waves of good wash over me. The full, free flow of life is running through my mind, my body and my affairs today.

I am relaxed in my mind, so I think clearly. As I am relaxed in my emotions, I have a feeling of love toward all people and toward my entire life. I am physically relaxed, so I am able to accomplish all tasks with tireless energy. I am relaxed in all that I do, so my world is now in perfect balance. Ease, order and right action describe my life at all times. I am thankful that this is so.

3

❖ ❖ ❖

Something Wonderful
Is About to Happen

The boasts and jests of the fishermen filled the air as the live-bait boat pushed out into the foggy Santa Barbara channel. There was much frenzied preparing of tackle and comparing of notes on how to best lure the reluctant fish out of the sea.

Quietest of those aboard were Bernice and myself. We were fresh from New York, and eagerly looking forward to this fishing trip in the beautiful California city where we had come to make our home. We didn't know much about fishing, but we were eager to learn.

The more experienced fishermen were generous with their help and advice, even though our rented tackle was the object of much joking. I openly expressed my doubts about catching anything. Later, I went so far as to say that I didn't care whether I caught any fish or not.

"You ought to be ashamed of yourself," my wife said. "Where is your faith? Of course you won't catch anything if you don't expect to. Now you start thinking right now about catching some fish. I'm starved for some."

Overhearing this remark about faith, several of the fishermen observed that it was a pretty poor substitute for good tackle and fishing skill. Bernice just laughed and retreated to her place near the rail, where she focused her attention on fishing.

An hour went by without anything happening. Impatiently, the experienced fishermen directed the skipper to move from one location to another in search of better results. Nothing seemed to help. The grumbling of the fishermen became louder. I myself was bored and said so. But one person said nothing—my wife kept her attention focused on her lines.

Suddenly, Bernice caught a beautiful fish! The fishermen cheered and congratulated her. Then she caught a second fish, then a third and fourth. The congratulations were now less enthusiastic. The fishermen were becoming a trifle jealous at being outdone by a woman.

Going to her, I said, "You know, everyone is getting annoyed because you're catching all the fish and they're not catching any. What are you doing?"

"Nothing," she smiled sweetly. "I'm just seeing fish coming along and going for my hook."

Returning to my place, I dropped my hook in the water and tried her technique myself. I visualized the biggest fish in the bay on the end of my line. In a few minutes there was a mighty tug and I hauled in what later took the prize as the biggest fish of the day.

Later, as we ate our catch, I was pondering Bernice's success where the old campaigners had failed. The answer suddenly hit me right between the eyes. *She expected to catch fish.*

THE POWER OF EXPECTANCY

The parallel between this simple story and many subsequent events in our lives convinced me that we get from life just about what we expect to get. Actually, the inner attitude of expectancy and the outer results always match each other exactly. Expectancy in our minds is the cause of everything that happens in our lives—both good and bad. How many times do we say, "I knew that would happen!" when something disastrous befalls us? And when something good happens, how often do we say, "I just knew that would come true"?

We are right both times. What we expect always happens. As we learn to discipline our minds, our job is to be sure that what we are expecting is what we *want* to experience. Powerful forces are set in operation by our attitudes of expectation. And these productive attitudes can be cultivated.

How to Build an Attitude of Expectancy

Again I use Bernice Curtis as an example. She awakened each morning saying, "I can't wait to find out what wonderful things are in store for me today." Of course, she had problems just as everyone had, but this cultivated attitude of the expectation of good constantly releases the power that creates good. When we look for the best in everything and in every situation, we automatically find it.

By minimizing the negative aspects of a situation and multiplying in our minds the good ones, we are constantly gaining and growing.

To put it another way, life is full of fish waiting to be caught by those who expect to catch them. The telephone, for instance, can help us build an attitude of expectancy. Whenever it rings, no matter how disturbing it may be, simply say: "I wonder who is calling me with good news?"

This attitude has a powerful effect upon the mind, and since the cause behind all things is mental, eventually a mind that is constantly attuned to good can only experience good.

Conditioning Yourself to Accept Good

Since the purpose of this book is to condition our minds to accept the mental attitudes enabling us to demonstrate more good in our lives, it is important that we expect this book to help us. I promise you that you will double your present capacity for living and experiencing good if you follow through with them. But these twelve basic attitudes are guides that can help us only *if we are willing to help ourselves.*

One excellent daily attitude conditioner that I have found effective is this simple statement: *I anticipate all impending events with enthusiasm and expectation of good.*

Memorize this statement and repeat it several times each day; it will condition your mind to eagerly expect good. If you look for good, you will find good, even though the situation of the moment seems unpromising or unpleasant. Even if you don't like what you see, train yourself to see what you *would like to see*. If you keep it up, you will be amazed to find that the situation really will change!

Build Expectancy Through Prayer

Following one of my lectures during which I discussed the principles of scientific prayer treatment, an elderly, rather heavyset woman came to Bernice and me. She asked for help with a physical condition—her abdomen was distended and painful, and surgery had been recommended.

During my talk I had pointed out how actual physical healing could be brought about through scientific prayer.

"Do you think prayer treatment could help me?" she asked.

"Let me ask you just one thing," Bernice replied. "Do you believe it can?"

"Yes ma'am, I do," she replied.

"Then you will be helped," Bernice said.

Having agreed to do daily prayer treatment for the lady, we did not see her again until the next week's lecture. She could hardly wait to tell us what had happened.

"Look at me, just look at me!" she exclaimed as she parted her coat and spun around. "I haven't been able to get this dress on for two years! My waist is almost down to normal and I feel just fine!"

"That's wonderful," Bernice said. "Tell us about it."

"Well, I just decided that I wasn't going to worry any more about my condition. I said to myself, 'I expect to be healed. God and Dr. and Mrs. Curtis are taking care of everything so I don't have to worry!' And do you know something—my stomach started acting up something terrible! There were the most awful mumbling and growlings and the pain was something fierce—but I just hung on. I said, 'I don't know what's going on here, but I know it's good.' Pretty soon it stopped—and now just look at me."

Our elderly friend again displayed her streamlined figure with youthful enthusiasm. We continued our treatment work for her for several weeks until a completely normal condition was restored.

The point of this story is simply this: *the lady expected to be healed.*" There can be no healing without the expectation of healing. What is the point of praying if we don't expect the prayer to be answered? Whenever Jesus was asked for help, he always asked, "Do you believe?" And when the supplicant answered affirmatively, he blessed him saying, "Thy faith hath made thee whole"—indicating that the attitude of expectancy on the part of the patient was the *real* prayer and its answer. This cannot be too strongly stressed. *The answer to the prayer is in our attitude of expectancy and faith when we pray.*

Expectant Attitudes Are Healing Attitudes

The miraculous accomplishments attributed to Jesus and other great spiritual teachers are the result of a complete attitude of expectation in their own minds. Jesus regularly addressed the Father with expectation of good *already* received. There was never any doubt in his mind. He said, "What things soever ye desire, when ye pray, believe that ye receive them, and ye shall have them."

Another principle of expectation is that there is that which obeys us *when we expect to be obeyed.* Such expectation of obedience gives a person an unmistakable air of authority. The person who expects results from his word always speaks quietly—firmly, yes, but softly, too, because there is no need for force or loudness when we understand this power. When Jesus spoke, people believed him. Why? *Because he expected to be believed.*

Dr. George M. Lamsa, the noted translator of the Bible from the original Aramaic, told the story of his personal experiences with spiritual and mental healing as a boy in Assyria. Before World War I, Dr. Lamsa's people retained the customs and way of life of Biblical times. In their simple culture, disease was unknown prior to the inroads of Western civilization. They accepted health as the normal condition. They *expected* to be healthy. In the case of physical indisposition of any kind, they went to see the only doctor they knew—the holy man who healed them through explanations and prayer. They never failed—not because of any unusual powers or gifts on the part of the healer, but because *the patient expected to be healed.*

Doctors tell of the power of expectancy in surgical cases, even going so far as to say that when *a patient expects to recover, he does. When he expects to or wants to die, he usually does.* Our attitudes of expectancy release a dynamic power which works in direct accord with the constructive or destructive aspects of our inner consciousness.

The Damage That Negative Thinking Can Do

We are all familiar with what happens when we say such things as:

1. "What a cold I'm going to have in the morning."
2. "After this workout I'll be so stiff I won't be able to move!"
3. "I wish we didn't have to go—we'll have a terrible time."
4. "There's going to be trouble. I can feel it."
5. "I'll never have enough time to do all the things I have to do."
6. "I can never get along with so-and-so. What a jerk he is."

What happens? You guessed it. The person *did* get a cold in the morning. He *was* stiff after the workout. They *did* have a terrible time when they went. There *was* trouble, and so on.

If you find that you are thinking negatively, reverse the process and start building constructive attitudes, thereby releasing the thought energy for constructive purposes. Now let's turn the above statements around, and say:

1. "I'll certainly be glad to get out of these wet clothes and into a hot bath."
2. "This is fun. I must get more exercise."
3. "I'm rather looking forward to this evening. We should learn a lot."
4. "I think this situation can be straightened out."
5. "This schedule may be a little tight, but I'll make it."
6. "So-and-so isn't so bad once you get to know him. Just needs a little experience."

WE GET WHAT WE EXPECT

Abraham Lincoln once said, "People are just about as happy as they expect to be." In other words, we attract and experience what we steadily expect. This attitude of expectancy, which is accepted by the subconscious mind, will be what produces results in our lives. We may *say* we believe a certain thing, that we expect certain results, or that we have faith in the working out of good in our lives, but unless our conviction goes deeper than just a surface statement, all our hopes and wishes will come to nothing.

Of course, mere wishing and wanting are not enough. Wishing must grow into a faith that what we have accepted *internally* must appear *externally.* Keep before you always the image of what you want to experience—see it, feel it, live it, love it, develop in your mind the mood of already having your cherished dream—then act from this viewpoint.

A 5-Point Expectancy Goal-Guide

1. *Success:* Do you want to be successful? Clarify in your mind what spells success for you, then live every moment in the expectancy of success. Think success. Feel successful. Act successful. Talk success. Do those things which indicate success, but you must first expect that results will follow! Have faith in the validity of your dreams, and faith in the working of the creative process that will make them come true.

2. *Happiness:* Do you want to be happy? Expect good everywhere. Live in constant anticipation that something wonderful is about to happen. Turn your thoughts toward those things which produce happiness. Avoid dwelling upon trouble, conflict and ugliness. Do those things which produce happiness for others. Give of yourself. Expect people to be good to you. Expect to have a good time living. These are the seeds of happiness. And who ever planted a good seed without expecting to reap a good harvest?

3. *Prosperity:* Do you want to be prosperous, to have plenty of all the good things of life? Who doesn't? You will have them if you expect them, and then follow through and do the things that are neces-

sary to bring them about. There is no lack in the universal storehouse. We experience lack, but this is the result of our limited concepts and our expectation of lack. Prosperity is first a state of mind; then money, possessions, and ease and freedom in their use appear in our world. What do you expect from life? Claim it and it is yours.

4. *Health:* Do you want to be healthy? Of course you do. Then expect this body of yours to be a perfectly functioning, balanced instrument. Expect it to do its job. Then take care of it by feeding, exercising, grooming and resting it properly, and nature will do the rest. Expect your body to heal itself and to grow and mature normally. Vitality and energy surge through your body when your spiritual, mental, emotional and physical aspects are all attuned to health. Disease is successfully resisted and age becomes a myth when you expect to be always young and always healthy. Make health a constant habit.

5. *Love and friendship:* Lonely people expect to be lonely. Usually self-centered and withdrawn, they subconsciously expect people to avoid them. They don't like themselves, so they don't see how anyone could possibly like them. On the contrary, the popular person never thinks about whether people are going to like him or not. He likes people, so they naturally like him. He gives of himself and people respond by giving of themselves. He is warm and pleasant to others, and they respond warmly and pleasantly to him. To have love and friendship, we must first give it. Expect people to like you and they will, provided you like them.

I remember an occasion as a boy when I was fortunate enough to win a public speaking contest. After basking in the applause of the audience, I hurried home for further praise from my parents. When I got there, however, very little was said. Finally I burst out: "Well, aren't you going to say something? You were there. What did you think of it? I won, you know."

Surprised, my father looked up from his paper. "Why of course, you did, son. Why shouldn't you win? You were the best speaker. We expected you to win."

During my athletic years, I remember well how silent our coach was when the team failed to live up to expectations in a crucial game. I also remember how we would silently resolve to correct our weaknesses so that we could win the next time and not let down the coach and fans who expected so much from us. *The expectations of others spur us on to our best efforts.*

"Remember, now you have two lives to live—one of them for him." I will never forget those words. They dug into my heart as painfully as the fingers of the boy's father dug into my shoulder. He had sobbed out the words.

It was just after the funeral of this man's son. He had been killed when he had come hurtling out of a blind alley and crashed into the side of the truck I was driving. Stricken by the tragedy, I had plunged into the deepest despair. But the boy's father had unwittingly shown me a way to atone for the guilt I could not help feeling. *I was expected to make up for the loss of that boy's life by doing more with my own life.*

That was more than sixty years ago, but as I have come to know more about the psychological working of the human soul, I know that my life has been deeply motivated by the father's grief-stricken plea of expectation. In his way, he was forgiving me by expecting a lot from me. I have often wished I could be free from that responsibility. For years, it created an inner pressure which would never let me rest; but this kind of pressure, properly channeled, can be the force which often leads us to our greatest accomplishments. Whatever success I may have had, I am sure is due in part to this experience years ago. It is my sincere hope that in helping others, I am in some measure making up for the loss of that boy's life.

We will always do our best to live up to the expectations of others. We have a natural abhorrence of letting anyone down.

Expect the Right Thing and It Will Come to You

At the start of this book I told you how I found my way back to purposeful living through the study of scientific principles of truth. But it didn't happen "just like that." I had a lot of help.

For several months I had attended Dr. Raymond Barker's class lectures in New York, absorbing the challenging inspiration of the basic principles of the Science of Mind. After class one day, I passed Dr. Barker in the hall as I was leaving. Stopping me, he put his arm across my shoulders and said, "Curtis, you ought to come into this work. You'd be great at it. I believe you could be one of the top men in the field in five years."

"Who, me?" I asked. Dr. Barker nodded. When he was gone, I felt as if he had left me there with a live grenade in my hand.

Entering the sort of work Dr. Barker was in had never entered my mind. Why should it? I was doing all right—well, most of the time anyway. Television was starting to roll in New York and I was in demand as an actor. I was averaging at least two programs every week, together with free-lance motion picture work. Money was rolling in, and greasepaint was still in my blood.

"Why, Dr. Barker must be out of his mind," I decided, and hurried along to my TV rehearsal.

But I had failed to recognize the power of the creative expectancy that Dr. Barker had planted. Little did I suspect what was in store for me.

I continued my studies, making an honest effort to grasp the principles of scientific truth. I wasn't making much progress, but I kept at it, trying to get used to this new way of thinking.

One day I was sitting in Dr. Barker's class, thinking about the points he was covering, when suddenly something clicked in my mind. In that instant I understood what he was talking about.

At the same time, I knew that I must enter this work. I felt as if nothing else was important. I wanted to devote my life to teaching others how to help themselves by applying spiritual principles to their lives.

Within a month I was speaking regularly each week. I was on my way. All of this happened within a few months after Dr. Barker dropped the new idea into my mind. The fact that I was interested, and had long been seeking a more creative avenue of expression than acting, had caused the seed of Dr. Barker's idea to take a hold in my subconscious mind. The principle is this: *When the subconscious mind accepts an idea, the inner creative power works to bring it to completion whether you are consciously thinking about it or not.*

After that, things started to move rapidly in my life. I had clarified my objective and nourished it with my *expectation* of achievement. In a later chapter, I will show you how this came about, but right now I wish to point out that it was the suggestion of a positive idea which led me to expect something of myself—something I had not even thought about before.

Demonstrating a Home

A number of years ago Bernice and I spent most of one summer at the shore on Long Island, spending our time in study and meditation, and in sifting our ideas and planning our future.

"What are you building?" I asked one day as my wife sat gazing out toward the horizon.

"Our home," she answered.

"What's it like?" I questioned.

"Oh, it's beautiful!" she exclaimed. "It's low and spread out, with plenty of room, and with glass windows all around. There's a view from every room. It's up on a high place, with still higher mountains rising back of it, and stretching out before it is a beautiful green valley leading down to the sea."

"Boy, you really have an imagination," I observed. "Now where do you think you're going to find a house like that?"

"We're not going to find it, we're going to build it—remember?"

"Where?"

"I don't know yet, but we'll know when we find it."

"Well, the only place I know where you could have a house like that is California," I observed.

"Then I guess we'll have to go there," Bernice concluded.

I saw no chance then of returning to California in the near future. My roots were now firmly established in the East. I had my television, stage, and radio commitments, as well as my lecturing work.

But I was reckoning without the power of expectancy that was working in both my wife and myself on three specific points:

1. She really expected to have just such a house.
2. I subconsciously expected to return to California some day.

3. I knew I was going to become a success in my new work as a minister and teacher of the Science of Mind.

Not quite three years later, Bernice and I had had our ministry in the Church of Religious Science in Santa Barbara for a little over one year. The series of events that brought about the move even now seem almost unbelievable. (I will tell more about them in later chapters.) We were happy in our work and we loved California. One morning Bernice awakened with the somewhat startling statement: "Today I am going out to find the place where we are going to build our house."

"To build what house?" I asked.

"Our house—our California home. It's time, don't you think?"

"What are you planning to use for money?" I inquired. The salary of a small-town minister hadn't exactly supported us in the style to which we had long been accustomed in New York.

"Now no negative thinking, Reverend!" she retorted. "I'm not going to have anybody interfering with my dream. We'll have what we need when we need it. Don't you think God wants us to have our home?"

"It never occurred to me that He was thinking about it," I replied. "I thought that was up to us."

"Oh, ye of little faith—," my wife admonished.

"All right, then, I'm all in favor of the idea. But will you tell me where the money is coming from?"

"You're going to go out and earn it. I feel a good picture coming on."

My wife was referring to the possibility of my getting a part in a motion picture. Since coming to Santa Barbara, I had supplemented my minister's income by commuting to Hollywood for an occasional motion picture or television film assignment. How grateful we were for my long-time acting profession, which was providing the wherewithal for me to switch over into my new profession while I was getting apprenticeship experience in a small church.

"Now, let's do our treatment work," Bernice said as we finished our breakfast. "I want to get started. I just know this is going to be a very important day."

And so we worshiped and treated together for the next half-hour. "Treatment" is the name for scientific, affirmative prayer. Treatment is the act and process of accepting an affirmative idea. Treatment is mental, spiritual and emotional unification with that idea.

In addition, treatment is the process of conditioning the deeper mind to accept and produce your desire or objective. It is a journey in consciousness wherein we move from where we are to where we want to be. Treatment is also the means whereby we reach inner conviction.

This book is about treatment in its broader sense. In our first chapter we started with relaxation, and in this one we are learning how to build an attitude of expectation, whereby we have a positive starting point toward the attainment of our goals and desires. If a person doesn't expect to succeed, he cannot help but fail. If you do not expect to be healed, you will remain ill until the mind develops an attitude of expectancy.

It is our purpose to help you live effectively through such treatment. With it, you will be able to solve your problems, heal your illnesses, establish abundance and freedom in your life, achieve your objectives, and build within yourself those qualities which represent the spiritually developed, emotionally mature, and well-balanced individual.

How to Use This Book with Maximum Effectiveness

There is no short cut to achievement and attainment in life. The process of growth cannot be skipped or forced, but it can certainly be assisted. That is what this book is for. It is a tool to help us release the inner creative power and energy so that it may produce good in our lives. Study these chapters diligently as they build each attitude necessary to accomplishment. A journey up the twelve steps of the Ladder of Accomplishment (given below) twice a day will bring results beyond your fondest expectations.

Use also the "Guides to Life" at the end of each chapter to get you started. These will focus your mind and get the creative process under way. After you become familiar with the process you will want to build your own attitude in your own words. But as you align yourself by this technique, be sure to cover all of the steps on the Ladder of Accomplishment, no matter how little time you have to spend. Cover them all, if only to review them in your mind. Fix them in your mind right now.

Here is a sample of how to use the twelve steps for general personal attunement and development:

THE LADDER OF ACCOMPLISHMENT

Align yourself with the twelve creative mental and emotional ideas. Get quiet inside and let your mind dwell upon them. Speak in simple direct statements with a feeling of conviction that what you are saying is really true. The subconscious mind thus accepts the suggestions presented to it and works to produce the results in our world.

1. *Relaxation*

Quietly now I release myself from all outer concern. I let my mind go free as I relax completely. I am relaxed physically, mentally and emotionally. I am free from all pressures and tensions. I am attuned to the free, full flow of life moving through my entire being. I let go and I let God take over. I am now cooperating with the creative process. All resistance is dissolved and I am ready for constructive action.

2. *Expectation*

I expect the best of life today. I expect to do my best and I expect the best from other people. I expect the harmonious and beneficial working out of every situation. I expect to give happiness. I expect good health in my mind, my body and my world of affairs. I expect an abundance of all things. I have more than enough to meet all my requirements. I thrill to the expectancy of living life fully today.

3. *Recognition*

There is one life, one Infinite Intelligence at the center of all things. Today I recognize the presence of a great loving power flowing through all creation. I feel this presence in every part of my being. I am aware of law and order back of all manifestation. I enjoy the prolific spontaneous beauty in all of nature. I know there is a cause back of every effect. I am convinced that there is One Cause back of all things. I recognize the privilege and potential of life. I know there is more to know than anyone has ever known. I let my mind expand into infinity today.

4. *Unification*

Whatever life is, I am living it. Whatever God is, I am expressing It. Whatever truth is, I embody it. I am an individual expression of the great mystery of life. I am one with all life. I am one with all people. I am unified with the Great Cause which is the Creator of all living things. I am a brother to every living thing. I embody the spark of divinity. My mind is my use of the One Mind. My soul is one with the Soul of the Universe. I can never be alone. All separation is dissolved as I attune myself to the oneness of life today.

5. *Dedication*

I am happy to be alive today. I know who I am, where I am going, and what I am here to do. I dedicate my life to the expression of good. I discover what I can do better than anything else, and I dedicate my talent, ability and efforts to the service of God and humanity. I am dedicated to living life fully today. I determine to do the best that I can at all times and in every situation. I find my right place in life and cooperate with the forces of growth. I love life and I love to live. I love people and I dedicate myself to helping make the world a better place in which to live. Happy, purposeful, abundant living is my dedication now.

6. Intention

I intend to succeed at anything and everything I undertake. I choose my objectives wisely and I intend to follow them through. I am filled with good intentions, and I do something about them. I intend to be a better person, and I start right now. I intend to express love and good will for all people, and I start right now. I intend to be happy, so no other thought ever enters my mind. I intend to be successful, so naturally I am successful. I have every intention of making this day the best day that I have ever lived. I intend to make my contribution to life today, and I start with these creative ideas.

7. Identification

I am one with the object of my desire. I live my objectives completely. I think, feel, breathe, taste, eat, drink and sleep my goals and objectives. I have a singleness of purpose. My life has focus and meaning as I provide a vital point into which the creative energy of life may flow. There is no place where God leaves off and I begin. I identify myself with the all-good which is God, so I become one with that good. I look like the constructive ideas in my mind. I act like someone who is identified with purpose, service and good deeds. This is the truth.

8. Conviction

There is no doubt in my mind today. I am convinced that I can go where I want to go, do what I want to do, and be what I want to be. This is my conviction, so it is true for me. My thought and my feeling blend together in forming my conviction. My conviction indicates the level of my faith. I carry the conviction of success. My subconscious mind is working for good because I have a constant conviction of good. I know all things are working out for the best. I know that right action is taking place in my plans and projects. I know I am growing; I know I am achieving. I do my best at all times to give to life the abundant good which I am convinced life gives to me.

9. *Realization*

Right here and right now, I realize the truth of these statements of good. I have convinced my subconscious that I am a spiritual being, just as the inspiration of my higher self gave the realization to my mind. I am free! I am whole! I am bright and clean and new. I have a fresh realization of the meaning of life. It is not what I get, it is what I give. It is not what people think of me, but what I feel for them! Today I realize that I live forever, but that this moment is the most important time of my life. All of my dreams have come true. I realize many things. I revel in the realization of my fondest expectations. I realize the goodness of life at all times.

10. *Projection*

I let my realization of good go before me and prepare the way. My atmosphere precedes me. What I am is visible from afar. My every thought, feeling and deed is a messenger and a servant. I proclaim the glad tidings from the housetops. I exude confidence, authority, strength and love. I know what I can do and people know that I can and will do it. My consciousness reaches to untold heights. My ideas, thoughts and undertakings are the channels through which my goodness is shared with the world. I hold nothing back, I share all that I have, and my consciousness reaches the stars. I am projected into total life today by the power of knowing.

11. *Action*

I must be about my creator's business. Today I get out and get going. I stir the stagnant waters and give them fresh release. I get to work and accomplish mighty deeds. I go where I need to go and do what I need to do. I flex my muscles and put them to work. I tackle the thing that cannot be done and I do it. I do not know what boredom and inactivity are. I am a doer. First I pray, then I act. I join thought, feeling and action into a mighty team of accomplishment. I won't sit around and wait. I work in harmony with the creative law of life today. Together we get things done. I am set to go. I act intelligently now.

12. *Cooperation*

I know that I can accomplish anything only when I am working in cooperation with the inner forces of life. I am merely a tool in the hands of a larger Doer. I do not resist life. I cooperate with life. I know that there is a larger purpose for me and I do everything I can do to attune my thoughts, feelings, and actions to this purpose. I flow with life. I feel its free, full flow through me now. I will never resist it. I revel in the release of spiritual power through my entire being. I let myself be used by something that is greater than I, and I do everything I can to assist its processes. I am on God's team and I know the meaning of teamwork now. And so it is.

Keep in mind that this is a general treatment of alignment and preparation for life. It is to be used each day. By using it, you are conditioning your mind with powerful ideas. There is no limit to the practical spiritual growth that can be achieved through the regular use of this conditioning. This Ladder of Accomplishment is in conscious alignment with the natural spiritual forces which are flowing through us. It is presented here as a guide for your use.

The guides at the end of each chapter are expanded treatments for each of the twelve key attitudes. As I have said, these guides form a technique whereby you may develop and strengthen each of these attitudes in your own consciousness. You may use my material verbatim in doing your own inner spiritual work, or you may prefer to improvise your own. The important thing is to pay some attention to developing those twelve inner attitudes of consciousness which form the basis for all accomplishment. *The level of the inner consciousness determines the level of the outer experience.*

As my wife and I worked together in treatment for our home that morning in Santa Barbara, we were using this principle. Remember, all we started with was an idea—and faith in the method for building our inner attitudes of mind toward a conviction that would allow it or cause it to manifest.

We were treating our total minds—the intellectual and emotional processes—to accept the idea of our new home. We were moving toward the conviction and acceptance of the idea *that the house was already ours.* When we finished our treatment our expectation was running high. We knew that something wonderful was about to happen.

It was not long in coming. Later that day, a phone call came from Cecil B. De Mille's office in Hollywood, asking me to be on hand the next morning for an interview with De Mille for a part in *The Ten Commandments.* At the time, Bernice was out scouring the hills back of Santa Barbara for the site for our new home. *The idea was unfolding. We were getting results.*

That evening we compared notes. My wife said that she had seen a "For Sale" sign in an area that would provide a beautiful home site.

When I revealed the prospect of my being in *The Ten Commandments,* her joy knew no bounds. We had expected something wonderful to happen, and it certainly looked as if it were going to. Our expectation was being increased by the favorable things which were happening. But we didn't stop there. We spent more time that evening strengthening our attitudes by using the twelve steps on the Ladder of Accomplishment.

We slept that night in calm assurance and deep inner expectancy that our affairs were in the best possible hands and that all was well.

The next day I was assigned the role of Mered in *The Ten Commandments.* The income from this made it possible to build our home, "The Land of Tomorrow," in Santa Barbara on the exact site that Bernice had spotted.

This example of a personal experience has doubtless shown you how you can be what you want to be, and do what you want to do, through the strengthening of your expectation of good. By using the techniques suggested you can recondition your subconscious mind to a completely affirmative attitude toward life. Remember that *our thoughts, attitudes and feelings are the parents of our experiences. We can consciously create circumstances, produce conditions, and control our own destiny by ordering and disciplining our minds.*

Let's start right now using our Daily Guide to Expectation.

DAILY GUIDE TO EXPECTATION

Today I expect the best in every situation. I don't know what is ahead for me today but I do know that it can only be good. I am a vital, dynamic center in the great creative scheme of things. I expect all of the riches and beauty of life to flow through my experience today. I recognize no limitation of any kind. I expect the most of myself at all times.

I expect to be happy today and always. I expect to be triumphant over every negative condition and situation. I expect to give my best to life and I expect life to return its best to me. I anticipate no evil; I accept only good. I am a happy person now.

I expect to be healthy today and throughout my life. I feel the free, full flow of life nourishing and building patterns of health in every part of my being. I am whole in body, mind and spirit. I expect to maintain this perfect balance of health at all times. I expect to function in perfect health through all the days of my long life. I expect to live forever. I am a native of eternity and I live to prove that this is so.

I expect to live in love and harmony with my world today. I love all of God's creatures and I am loved in return. I expect no conflict or difficulty at any time in any way. The way is prepared in love and I live it in love. I put my arms around the whole human race as my heart beats with the rhythm of love. I love life and I love to live. I expect the most of life today. I am thankful that this is so. And so it is.

4

❖ ❖ ❖

The Universe Is a Very Big Place

On the threshold of the new millennium, as in all ages past, man is seeking for an understanding of God and the universe in which we dwell. This search is often a desperate one, and despite all that has been written and spoken on the subject, we are not much closer to understanding the nature of ultimate reality than we ever were. In fact, the more we focus our attention on outer things, the farther we become separated from the Indwelling Presence, which is the Source of all experience. One of the purposes of this book is to unite us with our true inner potential—which, by whatever name we call it, is God.

Individual man is not entirely to blame for his confusion concerning God, and for the general turning away from the entire idea of a Supreme Deity. Religious concepts have probably done more to separate us from God than they have to unify and connect us with reality. Various degrees of agnosticism and atheism have been the inevitable result of man's difficulty in finding a spiritual concept that makes sense in the light of modern science and the demands of material experience.

One modern philosopher has stated, "There is no such thing as atheism, because the God which the atheist doesn't believe in isn't God in the first place." One could hardly blame an intelligent person for not believing in something which isn't true. And so the search for truth continues, as it always will, because *the ultimate purpose of life always has been, and must of necessity always be, to find the nature of God within ourselves.*

And except for a very few—the spiritually great in every age—often the meek and the lowly—man has not yet recognized that the kingdom of heaven is within him, although this truth has been proclaimed by teachers and seers for thousands of years. We always look elsewhere first. We are inquisitive creatures and we are always searching. Nothing has escaped man's inquiry, but every time our search leads us too deeply within ourselves we veer off on a tangent and start looking for the pearl of great price elsewhere.

Now, in this new age, we are searching in outer space. The genius and resourcefulness of science are being harnessed to speed up the search in, and conquest of, outer space.

But what happens? The more we discover, the less we find that we know. The farther we extend that which is known, the more we realize the challenge of the unknown. The more we are able to explain, the more aware we become of the fact that behind all phenomena is the unexplainable. The more dogmatic a scientist becomes on a certain point, the more surely he approaches the inevitable fact that just the opposite is also true. As witness our schoolbook axiom, "A straight line is the shortest distance between two points." This is true under ordinary relationships, but not necessarily when subject to the new dimensions of pure energy and outer space.

What has this to do with you and me? Let's look at it this way. If an Intelligence is the basis of all things, our approach must of necessity be through our own minds. When we learn to control and use our minds we will automatically control our experiences and our relationship to life.

Therefore, our next step upward on the Ladder of Accomplishment as we assist the creative process is *to recognize the Indwelling Power.* We are not going to do anything about directing it right now. We are not going to worry about how it works; we are simply going to recognize that it *does* work. We are not going to think about using it; we just know that we cannot help using this great life force, because it is all there is to use—*it is all there is.*

This attitude is *recognition*—coming to grips with that basic human need—*to find God.* This is not meant in any theological or religious sense. God is God no matter what man may think about such things. From our need and our search, we attempt to define God, if only to give us a clearer idea of what we are looking for. We remain balanced and constantly draw nearer to God when these definitions expand rather than limit our thought. This is what we are interested in here as we move up the Ladder of Accomplishment. In the final analysis, you must find God within yourself by finding what God means to you.

A small boy was drawing industriously upon the blackboard.

"What are you drawing?" his mother asked.

"A picture of God," he replied.

"But that's impossible. No one knows what God looks like," his mother said.

"They will when I finish," declared the boy with absolute confidence.

And so it is with us. We reveal the truth by the picture which emerges in our world from our thoughts and deeds.

We experience God as we become good. We become good by constantly recognizing good. Start right now to recognize good in everything. It is there. One only has to look for it. From such a habit of seeing the good in everything, one great spiritual leader, Mahatma Ghandi, was able to blend Eastern and Western spiritual philosophies together—the Sermon on the Mount and the Bhagavad-Gita became his twin Bibles. God was the ruling force in his life and the source of his dedication and power. He made no move without inner guidance, spending at least three hours each morning in meditation and prayer. His concept of God continued to grow throughout his life. He said, "I used to believe that God was Truth, but now, in my later years, I realize that *Truth is God.*" There is a vast difference.

We must learn to tell the difference between *that which is* and our own limited and mistaken ideas. One of this book's purposes is to help us break the bonds of ignorance, false ideas, and negative attitudes. This chapter's purpose is to teach us to recognize and use the power which enables us to do this.

All successful, happy men and women have an innate recognition and sense of oneness with a power that is greater than they are. A wise person intuitively recognizes that there is an infinite source from which all things flow. A person who recognizes and makes God an inseparable part of his life finds a balance and an inner peace which nothing else can give. People have always been aware that their strength flowed into them from a stream whose source was hidden.

It is obvious that we in the space age have only one real problem—our inability to find God. It must be that we are still looking in the wrong place.

A Sunday school teacher I know was explaining to her class one day that God is within each one of us. As she went on, the eyes of one little girl became wider and wider. She could hardly wait to get home with her tremendous discovery.

"Hey Mom!" she shouted. "Do you know I've got somebody walking around inside of me?"

And, of course, she was perfectly right.

Why then do we resist? Why is the idea of God so often unfashionable? It is not that we are not interested. We will always search for God. There is nothing in life to compare in importance with this quest, yet we avoid recognizing this.

The late Emmet Fox gave us a guide to practical spiritual living in his *Golden Key:* "Stop thinking about the difficulty, whatever it is, and think about God instead." This is the complete rule, and if only you will do this, the trouble—whatever it is—will disappear.

Now we have the problem of how to think about God. This is developed through practice, just like anything else. The twelve steps on our Ladder of Accomplishment help us to achieve our objective.

The Technique of Self-Emptying and God-Filling

In order to get on speaking terms with God, we must first get rid of the things within ourselves that do not belong there. What is left is God—pure, wholesome, perfect. Our twelve steps provide the basic technique for "self-emptying and God-filling." The pressures and problems of life bear in upon us until we are unable to see the larger picture, which *is* God.

In addition, when we are confronted with a problem or unpleasant situation it seems difficult to look through to the larger truth behind it. Yet this is exactly what we must do. We must recognize the potential of the perfect behind the imperfect. The extent to which we are able to do this will determine the change that we will be able to bring about in our lives.

A most attractive woman was in the audience during one of my lectures in Atlantic City a number of years ago. An inner beauty and radiance, which was noticed by everyone, shone from her.

"You are the most beautiful woman I have ever seen," I said as we shook hands after the lecture.

"Thank you, Dr. Curtis," she replied. "It means so much to hear you say that. I feel that I have been successful in using some of the things which you were talking about this evening—twelve steps on our Ladder of Accomplishment." She paused a moment, then said, "You say I am beautiful, but if you look again you will find that I'm really not—certainly not in the classic sense, anyway."

It was true. Feature by feature, she was not in the mold of the classic beauty, but the total picture was unmistakably beautiful.

"Would you be surprised if I told you that I was once called an 'ugly ducking?' " she asked.

"I certainly can't believe that!" I exclaimed.

"It is true. I was so plain that my family was actually ashamed of me. I was most sensitive about it. After suffering for years I finally decided to do something about it."

"Well, whatever you did was certainly a success," I said.

"Yes," she went on. "I think it worked."

"What did you do?" I asked curiously.

"One day as I looked into my mirror, I realized that if anything was to be done about my face, I would have to do it. So I started to see a beautiful face there instead of the all-too-familiar one. I pretended that the face I saw there was really beautiful. Every day I spent some time with my mirror and told myself that I was beautiful, that I was kind, and that God was shining through my face. People stopped calling me the ugly duckling, and I was happier than I had ever been. Occasionally people would compliment me upon my appearance, and I started to attract some attention from men. One or two even told me I was beautiful.

"At the same time, I started to act differently. I was nicer and kinder. I enjoyed doing things for other people. Finally one day I looked in my mirror and I saw something like you see today. Thank you for saying it is beautiful. Whatever I show comes from knowing that God is beautiful. Continue teaching people how to find God, Dr. Curtis. And if it will ever help, tell your audiences that you recognized the beauty of God through an ugly duckling you once knew."

I never saw the "ugly duckling" again, but she made a great impression upon me. I have never forgotten her example of what happens when you recognize that God is within you. I have told this story in hundreds of lectures and have experienced the miracle-working power of God-recognition in untold numbers of situations. There is no limit to the power of this wise statement: *Think of God instead of the problem, and the problem, whatever it is, will disappear.* This is the basis for all healing and accomplishment.

The self-emptying process is a matter of going to work upon ourselves for the purpose of changing for the better. Get below the surface of your mind and find out what really makes you tick. Then stand apart and try to see yourself as others see you. Be objective and ruthless in your self-analysis. Take a thorough inventory of your bad points—not your problems and difficulties, but the attitudes and character traits which are the causes of these problems. Be willing to surrender these negative traits and change them to opposite and constructive states of mind.

For instance, if you are afraid, start thinking about courage and faith. If you hate something or someone, start forgiving him. If you have a bad disposition, start being pleasant. If you are cruel, be kind. The results will show in greater happiness, improved health, richer experience, more harmonious relationships, and greater freedom on every level of life.

Surely, this is worth trying, isn't it? A recognition of God as the All-Good is essential. Sit down right now and make a list of all the good things that you can think of. I mean this literally. Get plenty of pencils and paper and give yourself plenty of time. It is a game that you will never tire of playing. Once you make it a habit you will never stop finding the good *in* things. *Recognition of good is recognition of God.*

As a person consistently develops constructive thoughts, feelings and attitudes, as we are doing here—and as you will continue to do throughout your life—something wonderful happens. The good that we dwell upon in our minds and hearts accumulates until we actually feel an inner awareness of something wonderful.

It is very simple: *As we raise our personal consciousness, we develop a universal consciousness of God.* The Bible says, "Draw nigh unto Him, and He will draw nigh unto thee." This is a very real experience, and is automatic when we develop the inner life to a high enough level of consciousness, as we can reasonably expect to do by progressing along the lines suggested by our twelve steps. And prayer can help us do this.

Prayer is a matter of talking to God. Make your prayer exactly that. Speak, think, feel—pray in your own language and from your own mind and heart. Your every thought and feeling is a prayer, *and prayer is always answered,* in terms of what was *in* the prayer.

People are apt to use various means to maintain their personal relationship with God. A friend of mine calls God "the Old Man," and relies upon Him completely. If he is working on a project he says, "The Old Man will help me." Or if he needs something he affirms, "The Old Man knows I need it; it will be there."

Irreverent? I don't think so. My friend knows what Jesus knew when he said, "The Father knows what things you have need of before you ask." My friend lives and works in the world. He is practical and realistic in everything he does, and can drive a hard bargain in a business deal. To be sure, he has problems, as do the rest of us, but somehow they don't bother him. He is really living on a different level. He is operating on a different wave length, tuned in on a higher frequency. *He has been touched by God, and when this happens a man is never the same.*

And this will happen to you. It happens to all of us. We never know just when, but it must. Let me tell you, for example, how it happened to me.

As I have said, my hospital experience had a profound effect upon me. Serious and painful though it was, my suffering brought me to a place where I saw that I must change. I knew that, then and there, I had to give up all that was false, and make an effort to attune myself to that which was true.

In my delirium, I saw clearly that one way led to death, the other to life. I wanted to live. And in a flash of insight, when God's mind filled my own, I saw the whole picture and what I must do. It was simple, and even though at that time my desire to live was purely selfish, *I was touched by God.*

One night, several days after the accident in which the boy was killed, my soul was crying out for reassurance. I had been unable to find it either from prayers, friends, parents or ministers. It was like wrestling with a devil; there seemed to be no light or help anywhere. Of course, in my suffering, I felt very sorry for myself. Small wonder that I lost sight of the larger picture—God.

While I was in this frame of mind, I stopped in front of a church and stood gazing up at the Cross. I did so somewhat superstitiously, hoping that I could get some symbol—perhaps of suffering, pain, I did not know just what—with which I could identify completely.

Suddenly I seemed to see a figure on the Cross, and a stray beam of light slanting across it. It was like a ray of hope for me. I knew then that I needed to talk to someone who would understand. Although it was two o'clock in the morning. I knocked on the door of the parsonage, where a light was still burning.

"Well, what's the problem?" the priest asked as he opened the door. "Come in and tell me about it."

I had never talked to a priest before. In fact, I was a bit shocked when I noted that, collar off and in his shirt sleeves, the good father was relaxing with a drink and a cigarette.

But the priest put me completely at ease. "Sit down, son," he invited. "It looks like we have some talking to do. Here, take your coat off. Make yourself comfortable. Cigarette? How about a drink?"

I took the cigarette. I always felt a little guilty about it, but I did smoke occasionally. But a drink! I declined and started to pour out my story to my patient listener. He heard me out; then he started to tell me about God. I don't remember the exact words, but what he said warmed me—just as did the drink which I had finally accepted. I often laugh when I recall that I got my first real taste of God and my first taste of whiskey at the same time.

I have always been grateful to that small-town priest who talked so sensibly to me on that troubled night long ago. He helped me find my way by reaffirming that there was a God when I had begun to doubt it. The last time I saw him he left me with this benediction: "Remember, all roads lead to God!"

Some roads are just more winding and tortuous than others, that's all. But we do all eventually get there.

A very practical way to "practice the Presence" in daily life is by constantly affirming, "Where the problem seems to be, God is already there." It is amazing what messes we can get into when we forget this principle, but it is equally amazing—and gratifying—to see the tremendous results which accrue when we remember to use it.

Shortly after I began to get a glimmer of what Dr. Barker and my other teachers were talking about in the Science of Mind philosophy, I went through a series of experiences which can only be described as a kind of rebirth. In fact, this awakening—the finding of God—is called "rebirth" throughout spiritual literature. Jesus said, "Except a man be born again, he cannot see the kingdom of God." Paul speaks of being reborn, and vividly describes his own awakening when he was stricken blind on the road to Damascus. "Seeing the Light" also plays a prominent part in the accounts of many individuals' awakening; in fact some people actually see a light and are greatly affected by it. Others, in their growing recognition of God, have a deep and thrilling feeling of inner awareness and excitement. Still others are suffused with a vast feeling of peace and well-being.

In my own case, I experienced all of these symptoms most vividly; and then, as now, I was only beginning to get a glimmer of true reality. The universe is a very big place and the wonders of it are infinite. By our recognition of a Higher Power, and our application of what we learn from it, each of us makes his own penetration into the vastness of inner space.

During this early period, I was once awakened in the middle of the night by a deep inner stirring and a tingling feeling in my solar plexus, accompanied by breathlessness. At the same time the room was filled with a soft glow of light. I lay still on my bed drinking in the air with great gulps, but otherwise completely swept up in the ecstasy of the experience. My body became light and tingled all over as if an electric charge were going through it. I was thrilled and excited, but completely without fear.

My heart beat rapidly and I continued to breathe rapidly and deeply, as if trying to fill myself with the magnificence which surrounded me. I lay there in this state for several hours, my mind completely free, revelling in the joyous sense of elation and freedom. Finally, as the first light of dawn started to appear, the other light faded, and I sank into a deep sleep, exhausted but completely happy and relaxed. It was a truly transforming experience.

This experience was repeated almost nightly over a period of several months. I was studying intensively during this time, learning about meditation and a scientific prayer treatment, yet I had never been able to *consciously* bring about the experience. It came of itself when I was asleep, and I was awakened to participate in it. My life was changed as my inner awareness expanded.

Your own recognition of God may or may not be accompanied by unusual experiences. It has been several years since mine, and I have never had one like it since, even though I have approached it several times.

Our goal on this rung of the Ladder of Accomplishment is a recognition of the Infinite Presence at all times and in all places. It will be there for you when you recognize it.

What Are the Seven Aspects of Spirit?

Thomas Troward, one of the early pioneers in mental science, described the aspects of Spirit as: Life, Love, Light, Power, Peace, Beauty and Joy.* Thought and meditation upon these aspects of the One develop a consciousness of recognition.

You can actually prove this to yourself. Become very quiet and let your mind dwell upon these ideas, perhaps speaking your thoughts simply and quietly in order to keep your mind focused on them. Remember, our purpose in using this technique is to develop our recog-

---

* Troward, Thomas. CREATIVE PROCESS IN THE INDIVIDUAL, (London: L. N. Fowler & Co., Ltd., 1954).

nition of our inner life, which is Spirit. This cannot be hurried or forced. It is a way of life and requires regular practice.

Here are some suggested texts for Troward's Aspects of Spirit. Repeat these meditations slowly and with the greatest conviction you can muster, then feel the inner power glow into your whole being.

Life

There is life everywhere. This great invisible stream is flowing through me right now. I am one with the teeming abundance around me. I feel the stirring of life in every atom of my being. My thought is life in action. My heart pumps the stream of life through my body. My nervous system carries the electric currents of life through my entire being. I express life with every part of me. I look out upon my world and I see life everywhere. I am one with every living thing. The earth is teeming with the life that flows from the One Source, the fountain of all life. I love life and I love to live. I devote myself to living the abundant life on every level. I know that I have eternal life. I know that God's life is my life now. And so it is.

Love

Love is life in action. Love is the movement of good through all things. Love holds the universe together. Love makes all things possible. Only love makes life meaningful. Love is the urge of life to express itself. Love is the questing of my soul to join with its Source. Love is my recognition of and identification with life. I love because I live.

I live life and I love it. I love God indwelling in all things. I love my life and the great potential which I am. I love other people. I recognize and love the true self within each one. I love the living and growing things. I love my work, and I love the joys and experiences of life. I am in love with life and I express this love wherever I go. I express love in all that I do. I am love. And so it is.

Light

I open my eyes and I see light everywhere. Light is the visible evidence of the presence of Spirit—the Life Force and Substance. The forces of light quicken me today, stimulating my mind, purifying my emotions, and vitalizing my body. Light is energy speeded up, and I am filled with spiritual energy at all times. My entire being is filled with light. I am illumined from within. Light brings understanding to my mind and wisdom to my soul. Darkness is dissolved as I let my light shine forth. As I strive to become a good example, I am a beacon lighting the way for all to follow. I am a point of light within the mind of God. I embody and carry the light today. And so it is.

Power

My power comes from within. God is the source of my power. "The Father that dwelleth in me, He doeth the works." I am filled with invincible power. I recognize it, I feel it, I use it, and I cooperate with this inner power. As I channel my power wisely, I am equal to any task or situation. I am capable of doing whatever needs to be done. I am superior to any problem. I transcend all limitation. I have spiritual knowledge, and knowledge is power. Divine Power awaits my command. I speak the word and it is done. The creative engine of the universe is throbbing within me now. I am the custodian and the user of all the power there is. I am a powerful person because my power comes from God. And so it is.

Peace

I am at peace. My mind is attuned to infinite peacefulness. I am at peace. My body is quiet. I am at peace. My actions are balanced. I am at peace. My world is in order. I am at peace. My relationships are harmonious. I let all good things flow from my peaceful and quiet mind. As my mind is attuned to the Source of all peace, I experience peace in all that I do. I am still and I know that the power within is God. I am calm, cool and collected. I quiet the winds and the waves of life's storms. I am a messenger of peace. I share my peace with other people. My inner peace is my contribution to peace in my world. I am ever at peace. And so it is.

Beauty

I see beauty everywhere. I am immersed in beauty. I express beauty. I dwell only upon that which is beautiful. I mold my life into beautiful thoughts, beautiful feelings, and beautiful deeds. I am made in the image and likeness of that which is beautiful, so my true self must be beautiful. I devote my life to making this true. All nature is a mirror of beauty. All life is the expression of beauty. Growth is the movement of beauty. Every movement of my life is filled with beauty. I am surrounded with beauty because I am filled with beauty. Life is beautiful and I live it with beauty today. And so it is.

Joy

I am happy. I am free. I am filled with joy. I know that God has a sense of humor and I laugh loud and long with the joy of living. Joy is evidence of happiness. The teeming earth is bursting with joy. As the rose blooms, it joyously proclaims that it is glad to be a rose. As I sing and laugh my way through life, I am showing that I am glad to be alive. I am a joyous person. I spread joy wherever I go. My face is lighted with inner joy. My smile is a joyous sight for others. I have so much joy I can't contain it all, so I give it away to the whole world. I share my joy with everyone I meet. The world is a joyous place. I shout with joy today. And so it is.

After you have read these treatment-meditations, say them out loud until the ideas penetrate your subconscious. Really believe what you are saying. Every thought and word develops your recognition of God, because an understanding and an inner feeling of these seven basic aspects will move us closer to a true recognition of what God is.

Note that these exercises are part explanation, part affirmative prayer treatment. Their sole purpose is to expand our consciousness of recognition. The statements are made in the first person, because they are for *your* personal use. As you repeat these ideas with conviction and feeling, your mind accepts them, and they *are* true for you. That is why all such statements should be made in the present tense. Never postpone a desired good by shoving it into the future. Accept it *now*. Condition your mind to it *now*, and the details of manifestation will work out with proper timing.

MAKE "CONSTRUCTIVE BRAIN-WASHING" WORK FOR YOU

These exercises, together with similar ones throughout the book, and the Guides to Life at the end of each chapter, are a kind a "constructive brain-washing." They cannot help but bring good into your life. After you have become familiar with them, you will want to put similar ideas into your own words. As your inner recognition grows, your outer expression naturally expands. These exercises are for the purpose of getting you started in the right direction.

Meditation of some sort is necessary in developing our recognition of the Inner Presence. There are many ways to meditate, and each person usually develops his own, based upon the help given by a teacher in the early stages.

Basically, meditation is the process of being still and knowing something. Very few of us have any proficiency at this until we work to develop it. One primary purpose of meditation is to rid the mind of limiting ideas, and free it for new concepts. This naturally poses some difficulties because all ideas are limiting. Therefore, if we are to develop to our full potential, the first step in meditation is to empty the mind and free it from all thought. But can this be done? Is it possible to *think of nothing?* Should the mind be made a blank? If you try to do this, doesn't the very effort defeat your purpose? These are questions everyone asks about meditation. They cannot be answered by yes or no.

Each of us must find out for ourselves how to meditate, but the following exercise will start you on the right road. This exercise has gradually developed as a technique during years spent in the practice of meditation. Thousands of my students have enriched their lives by using it. Its primary purpose is to develop a sense of inner oneness. It is yours. Please use it.

A TECHNIQUE FOR PROPER MEDITATION

1. First, *relaxation.* Remember that every step in the Ladder of Accomplishment is preliminary to, and integrated with, each succeeding step. Relaxation always comes first. Use the techniques for relaxation given in Chapter 2. Become completely still outside and inside.

2. Second, *expectation.* Sharpen your mind. Bring it to a point of expectant awareness. Use the techniques and suggestions in Chapter 3. Repeat the "Guide to Expectation." Anticipate an exciting inner experience. Realize that something wonderful is about to happen.

3. Third, *recognition.* Close your eyes, but focus them at a spot at the center of your forehead. Imagine that a soft, bright light bulb is pressed against your forehead. This light fills your entire awareness and gives you a sense of complete peace. Think of nothing else. Let the light suffuse itself through your entire being, warming and cleansing you. You are at peace. You enjoy the light. "Let your eye be single and your whole body will be filled with light." Visualizing and identifying yourself with the light will quiet your mind completely and give you a focus so that your mind will not wander toward anything else. Remember, we are not trying to make anything happen. We are becoming receptive to the inner awareness of good. We are recognizing and unifying with our Higher Self; as the Bible puts it, "Be still, and know that I am God."

Remember, light is one of the aspects of Spirit, or God, so we dwell in the light and remain still as long as we choose. Soon there will be various colors and then images which will appear in the light. These vary with different people, but it is perfectly normal. These are merely surface reflections from your subconscious mind, or after-images from your visual nerves. Take time in complete quietness to let these wear off. The colors will progress from heavy dark colors, to grey, to dull red, then red, orange, yellow-gold, blue, and then pure white, back to where you started by visualizing the light bulb. This gradation of colors represents the progress of purification which is taking place within you.

Now visualize a triangle superimposed in the circle of light—an equilateral triangle, solid and dark, silhouetted in the light. Touch each point of the triangle, and keep it clearly focussed in your mind. Next, let all of your attention move toward the upward point of the triangle. This symbolizes the upward path—the natural progress toward growth and enlightenment. We are always moving from the broad base of things, upward to the pinnacle of light and inspiration. The triangle symbolizes this, and at the same time gives us a point of focus so that we may completely quiet the mind, making us more receptive to the recognition of the total picture of things—God.

As your attention is focussed at the peak of the triangle, visualize it as a snow-capped mountain; see yourself at the very summit, free and victorious. This is the mountain of life. The snow-capped summit represents enlightenment and attainment—the ultimate and assured goal of each of us. All roads lead up the mountain, tortuous and slow though the path may be. It may wind and turn, but it is always ascending, ever journeying through experience toward complete recognition of that which is: truth, fulfillment—God.

As we dwell upon these ideas during our meditation, using the symbols as suggested, we experience a growing recognition of the real meaning of things; and this, of course, is the purpose of life.

As you hold your attention upon the summit of the mountain during your meditation, noble and lofty ideas will fill your mind, and the recognition of many wonderful things will come to you. Hold your attention upon each idea, remaining free and relaxed, exerting no personal effort at all. If your attention wavers, bring it back by focussing upon the mountain, silhouetted against the circle of light, its snow-capped peak glistening majestically and inspiringly in the light of the true spiritual sun.

Before completing your meditation, travel around the three points of the triangle, connecting them with a perfect circle. The three points represent spirit, mind and body—the three-fold nature of man—and the circle represents the unification of your own consciousness. Our consciousness is our recognition of the Infinite Intelligence—the One which is God.

Such techniques as this one help to expand the individual understanding toward total recognition. Our Ladder of Accomplishment provides a guide for developing and maintaining those inner attitudes which integrate us and automatically produce order, harmony and happiness in our experience.

By meditating with this technique you will begin to recognize God in all things. Form the habit of making every waking moment your meditation and prayer. Formal techniques help to ingrain the habit of conscious recognition, but once it is ingrained, we recognize only good at all times. We perceive the causes and reasons behind all happenings. Even problems and difficulties are means by which our good comes to us. There is no evil—only good. What seems evil is only the absence of good. The way to growth and attainment is to expand our consciousness of good.

Remember that this inner recognition of good automatically brings about good in our world. That is the Law. All we need to do is recognize this principle and discipline ourselves to live by it.

Now, go back over this chapter and review the main points in your mind, paying particular attention to the section on the seven aspects of Spirit, and practicing the meditational technique suggested.

Here is your Daily Guide to Recognition:

DAILY GUIDE TO RECOGNITION

Today I recognize the presence of God in all things and in all places. I see only good everywhere. I recognize God at the center of every person I meet. I look out upon my world and find it very good indeed. I dwell in the kingdom of heaven and I see its glories reflected from everything in life. All of nature expresses the wonder that is God. Every living thing is singing the praises of the Most High. Every atom of substance has its place in the great scheme of things. I know that back of all things is the wholeness and perfection of the One Mind—the First Cause and the Creator of all things.

I recognize the presence of the Universal in every individual thing. I see God in the grain of sand, and I feel eternity in the ticking of every second. Each blade of grass expresses the handiwork of the Master Craftsman. Nature is the textbook which reveals to me the secrets of life. I recognize the imprints of Divinity everywhere I look.

I recognize myself as a spiritual being. I am made in the image and likeness of God. Whatever God is I am expressing It. Whatever life is, I am living it. Whatever truth is, I am knowing it. Whatever good is, I embody it. My mind, my emotions, and my body are all attuned to the spiritual wholeness within me. I am a whole being. Perfection dwells in me. Divine energy flows through me, as I draw upon the Infinite Source. I am integrated with That which is greater than I. I am unified with all good. I am a whole person. I am complete.

The recognition of God goes before me making whole and complete the pathway of my experience. "I will fear no evil. For Thou art with me. Thy rod and thy staff, they comfort me." I am at peace today because I recognize that God is the Presence and the Power in my life. And so it is.

5

One with All Life

I had just been given my first .22 rifle, and I reacted with the pleasure of any twelve-year-old boy when he has power placed in his hands. Although I was carefully instructed on its safety and use, I still wanted to shoot at everything in sight. Fenceposts and tin cans were peppered unmercifully, but the squirrels and hawks, my two legitimate prey, were always able to evade my marksmanship. One day while walking through a ploughed field, I saw a slight movement. I took aim, fired and ran toward my target. I had drawn my first blood! A tiny field sparrow lay very still, with a single drop of blood marking the place where the bullet had entered its body.

I was crushed by what I had done. It seemed so useless. The little bird which had been so gaily alive was now dead. I cried as I cradled it in my hand and pressed my cheek against its stiffening body. Slowly I trudged home, placed my prized rifle in the closet, and never touched it again. My days as a hunter were over. I simply could not kill.

It is this feeling of oneness with all life which has motivated one of the most remarkable men of our time, Albert Schweitzer. His basic philosophy, "reverence for life," expresses the universal language of love. Even though I did not know it, I was feeling love as I held the dead sparrow.

The fourth step on our Ladder of Accomplishment is *unification,* and deals with the mental and emotional attitudes of oneness, integration, strength and power. These all come from love. First we learned how to relax, then how to adopt an expectant attitude, and in the last chapter we developed the capacity to recognize God. Now in the present chapter we shall learn how to unify with this Power—become one with it. This process of identifying with the One Source is love.

Early in my training as a minister and spiritual practitioner, one of my teachers said to me: "Remember, the people who come to you are short on two things—love and understanding. Give them those and they will be healed." And it is true. Everyone is looking for something to end their feeling of separation and bring them back into their "Father's house." Love provides the concept of unity and wholeness which is the basis of any sound, sane and balanced approach to life. Without love we perish; with love we live joyously and abundantly.

There is the well-known story of the doctor's prescription tacked to the foot of the hospital nursery crib: "This baby is to be loved every two hours." Or the touching story of the nine-year-old girl in an orphanage who was observed slipping away one afternoon and going to a large oak tree near the grounds. Following her, one of the attendants found this note in childish scrawl hidden in the trunk: "Whoever finds this, I love you." We are unified with the Source of all being by learning how to give and to receive love.

Recently a veterinarian asked me to come with him while he went to one of his cages. He took out a small, woolly puppy and held it against his cheek for two or three minutes without a word. Then he said, "We almost lost that one. I couldn't find anything wrong with her, so I'm just loving her regularly and she is coming along fine."

Could it be that the world is dying from lack of love? Could it be that we hold the key to personal and world ills within our own hearts, and all we need to do is learn to love? It is my belief that this is true. This book is written for the purpose of showing us how to develop twelve basic constructive mental and emotional attitudes which add up to love for life. This over-all concept includes love to self, love to others, love of work, love of God—*unification*.

There are no shortcuts to achieving a sense of unification. But there are many ways to assist our upward progress. The twelve steps themselves explain and demonstrate some of these ways.

Actually, unification is primarily a matter of growth. The soul within us grows and evolves throughout eternity. We live forever through many lives, inhabiting our bodies, and eventually traversing the entire spectrum of experience on every level. We are one with the greater life on every level—spiritually, mentally and physically. Our souls are one with Spirit, our minds are one with the Infinite Intelligence, and our bodies are formed from the Universal Substance. Thus, we see how important it is to constantly work toward this goal of unification. Our twelve steps are the way we travel to attain integration and completion.

We have all had the experience of exhilaration which comes from a deep inner feeling of joy and power. The higher states of consciousness come sometimes when we least expect them, but their effect upon us can be profound if we listen and learn. Remember that everything happens for a reason, and whatever comes our way, we should ask, "What is the lesson here? What is this trying to teach me?"

I remember one such high moment of inspiration when I was a boy working on my father's farm near Spokane, Washington, many years ago. It lasted for less than half an hour, but the breakthrough into a freer and more comprehensive awareness was so intense that it has had a profound effect upon my life for over thirty years.

The spaciousness and loneliness of the rolling hills of a large wheat ranch give one plenty of space and time in which to dream.

Standing high on a hill one day, my mind seemed to encompass everything. It was as if the world were in me instead of me being in the world. I felt myself one with the clouds, the sky, and the limitless expanse of blue. I was more alive than I had ever been in my life, and I caught some magnificent glimpses of who and what I really was. I felt that there was nothing I couldn't be—nothing I couldn't do. It was as if I were being carried to the heights and allowed to see the whole picture, where before I was limited to only a small part. I was free and powerful; I was a man!

Even today, the whole experience often comes back to me, and I am recharged with the thrill and the energy of that brief experience so long ago. Many times in moments of stress I have recalled that moment, and the pressures have been washed away.

We should all have such experiences frequently—and we will learn to truly understand ourselves and use our inner capacities. We can live constantly in this elevated consciousness when we learn that the inner life is the reality—the cause; while the outer experiences are the projection—the effect.

One of the main lessons in this book is that this high state of consciousness—inner balance, harmony and authority—is our *normal state*. Anything less than that is subnormal. Yet, at the same time, we must realize that this ideal has not yet been achieved. This book develops a technique for traveling from where we are to where we want to be, up the twelve steps of the Ladder of Accomplishment, to the true realization of our potential on every level.

I have tried to show you how this technique has worked in my own life and the lives of others; and I will continue to do so in the chapters to come. I want you to believe that there is no limit to your capacity for achievement. Jesus said, "He that believeth in me, the works that I do shall he do also; and greater works than these shall he do."

Nowhere in his entire teaching does Jesus tell us anything that we *cannot* do. He simply asks, "Do you believe?" and then affirms, "According to your faith be it done unto you." He didn't ask the people what church they went to, or if they had sinned lately, or who their father was, or if they had bathed recently. He simply said, "According to your faith be it done unto you," teaching that something happened to bring our desires, hopes, dreams and thoughts into manifestation if we believed in ourselves. He taught further that to believe in oneself is to believe in God, and that when we are unified with God, all things are possible. As we have said, this process of unification is called *love*. With it all things are possible; without it, nothing is possible because, "God is love," and "Love is the fulfilling of the Law."

Now this is not a book about religion in its ordinary sense. A person's religion is the way one lives, and this book is about a way of life which I have found rewarding and fulfilling. I have no authority for its validity except to show you how it has worked in my life and in the lives of the many whom it has been my privilege to teach. I have thousands of letters in my files with reports of everything from instantaneous healings of so-called incurable diseases, to the accumulation of enough money to buy braces for little Susie's teeth. Each of these people, in his own way, has discovered how to unify himself with the Source of all power. And each has been able to do this through a process of personal discipline and practice.

That is the whole point: *It works.* That is actually all I know about it. When I have let it, it has worked in my life from the very beginning. It will do the same for you—if *you* let it.

The whole business of life becomes clear and simple when we take time to understand some of these elementary principles. All we have to do is know a few things, believe in them, live by them and sustain them by staying on the affirmative side of life by a simple process which Paul referred to when he said, "Pray without ceasing." For this book is really about prayer.

Our twelve steps on the Ladder of Accomplishment deal with the essential attitudes of continuous prayer. Everything we think or feel is our prayer. What we think and feel determines our experience. So our prayers are always answered—completely. "As man thinketh in his heart, so is he." The affirmative prayer formed by our twelve steps makes it possible for us to determine our experience by conditioning our subconscious mind with constructive thoughts and feelings. The twelve basic attitudes of this book, one of which we develop in each chapter, form the perfect prayer—the prayer that gets results.

To pray effectively in this way, let us gather our "disciples"—the twelve steps of this book—around us, thereby becoming a whole person, unified in spirit, mind and body. You can do it. I know you can. When I first started teaching, some of my friends and former associates were surprised, to say the least. One even exclaimed, "My God, if Curtis can become a minister, anyone can."

The point is, you can do anything you want to do if you can develop the *consciousness* of that thing. My friend was seeing the outer change without realizing that there had first been an inner change. And, of course, this inner change is the basis of any outer change.

I believe, along with other spiritual mind teachers, that it is possible for people to assist their spiritual unfolding—their inner change—by consciously cooperating with the spiritual power that lies within them. Whatever I can tell you about that process in this book is my contribution toward this end. My deepest prayer is that it may do for you what it has done for me.

Let's be very clear about one thing, however. It is not a short cut. It is a tool for you to use so that you can live more effectively. It assists the process of growth by integrating you as an individual and by unifying the various aspects of your being. The entire series of twelve steps forms a complete prayer when taken in sequence from beginning to end; also, each step is a prayer in itself. And remember, prayer is the process of unifying individuals with the Source of their being. Now, the twelve guides of this book form the basis for the practical modern religious philosophy which I teach. Make them your own and let your inner personal religion become the most important thing in your life. Above all, don't be afraid to get your life on a constructive spiritual basis just because you have been separated from God for a long time. Don't condemn yourself because you have made mistakes and have done foolish things in the past.

I often tell my audiences, "If there is any wrong that I haven't done at least once, I don't know what it is, so let's start from there. This teaching is for everybody, no matter what you have done, no matter what your habits are, no matter what a mess you have made of things. So don't hold back just because you have done things to make you ashamed of yourself. Let's find out why you did those things, and when we change the reason, you will stop doing them. It's up to you. You can change if you want to and if you'll be honest with yourself. So let's get started. What do you say?"

In my own life, after the many years of struggling for things— riches, recognition, security—all without avail—I have found peace in simply knowing about the principles discussed in these chapters. And by actually applying them I probably have accumulated more satisfaction than those things I struggled to get would have brought me. The point is, there is something more to this business of living than just getting and having. We can all have the greater part if we want it. It is up to us. "Seek ye first the Kingdom of God, and His righteousness; and all these things shall be added unto you."

The process of unification is greatly assisted by an understanding of what we are—basically *spirit, mind* and *body.* This relationship is clearly shown by this diagram:

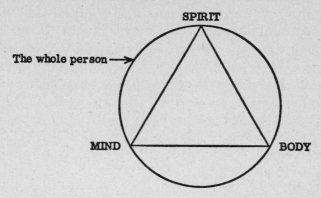

We can only be a whole person when we clearly recognize this basic unity. Spirit is the God-part within us. The Mind is our capacity to use it, and Body is what results from this use. The circle in the diagram represents the wholeness which results when we unify ourselves with the components of our makeup. The circle is the symbol of inner unity—the kingdom which Jesus talks about. When we condition our minds by developing the twelve basic mental attitudes, this comes about automatically.

Now, this unity is broken when we have an intense desire for something and become frustrated when we do not have it. Intense outer effort to attain our objective postpones its demonstration. Unless we first do our inner spiritual and mental work—unless we first accept our objective in inner consciousness—we will never attain it. Many times in life, our burning desire and intense struggle to attain our objective often separates us from that objective because we are constantly affirming that we do not have it. Our process leads us to the conviction that all things are incipient within us and will be demonstrated in our experience according to our recognition and our acceptance.

This conviction is perhaps the single most important step in finding happiness and peace of mind. An inner sense of unity with all life will bring it about. After this is attained, we will be much less concerned about praying for what we want. We will be much more interested in what we *need* for our *fulfillment* as a complete person. Our twelve steps actually form this circle of completion.

Right now we are building a consciousness of unity with all life. We express all of life at the point where we are. God, the Infinite Intelligence and energy, is pouring into us. Let us open up our consciousness to the influx of abundant life. Jesus said, "I am come that they might have life, and that they might have it more abundantly." Try to see yourself in relationship to God and to life in this basic diagram:

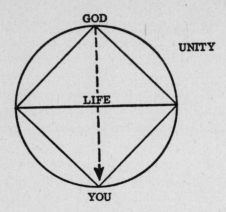

Since God-power is pouring into us through Life, it is up to us to live fully and abundantly, to be a whole person, and to live up to our full potential.

It is up to you. Let's do it right now.

DAILY GUIDE TO UNIFICATION

I am one with all life. All separation is dissolved as I realize that "I and my Father are one." I am one with nature. The elements of earth, air, fire and water are unified within me. I am a fluid part of God's total universe. I am one with all that is—one with all that has ever been or will ever be. Time and space blend into the one as I see and become one with the total picture.

I use my sense of unity and power to become a better person. I dissolve anything unlike the nature of God from my consciousness. I am a whole person. I am a complete being. This is my constant frame of reference. I do not depart from it for one second. I know who I am and where I am going. I am attuned to the full meaning of life. I have a job to do on myself and I do it.

There is no place in my life for the trivial or the second rate. My life is a living prayer. I contemplate the facts of life from the highest point of view. I am a good person and I am constantly becoming better. I am sustained by noble ideal and purpose. I constantly strive to do the best possible job of being myself. I know that I am a son of God and it "doth not yet appear what I shall be."

I give thanks for the abundance which is mine. I am heir to the total riches of the kingdom. I give thanks for life. I give thanks for myself. I give thanks for other people. I give thanks for the opportunity to live, to learn and to grow. I give thanks for the joy and the enthusiasm which activates my every thought, word and deed. I give thanks for the love which unifies, sustains and gives meaning to all things. I give thanks for the truth which makes me free. And so it is.

6

❖ ❖ ❖

Why Are We Alive?

"Who am I?"
"Where did I come from?"
"Why am I here?"
"Where am I going?"

Every one of us has asked these questions at one time or another. What we are at this particular moment is the living answer that we have reached concerning them. There is no final answer. Everyone must find their own. Some people find the answers early in life, while others must be shaped on the hard anvil of experience before they are capable of finding purpose and meaning in life. When our focus is centered upon doing what we came into this life to do, the results will take care of themselves. Our job is to do the best job of being ourselves that we can—and to do so with a complete release of any concern as to what results it will bring. Each person must find the creative spark within their heart and fan it into a living flame. Only then will the meaning of life become known to us.

Jesus, for one, never had any doubt as to why He was here and what He had to do. He said,

> "For this cause came I into the world, that I should bear witness unto the Truth. . . . I must be about my Father's business. . . . I am come that they might have life, and that they might have it more abundantly . . . And, if I be lifted up from the earth, I will draw all men unto me."

As we study the life of the carpenter of Nazareth, we are constantly impressed and inspired by His unswerving dedication to purpose and principle. He never compromised nor waivered in the guiding purpose of His life: to prove by living example that man is one with God. To accomplish this was reward enough for Him. He was not concerned with results. He was not discouraged when he was rejected. He remained true to His dedication when He was reviled, tortured and eventually killed. But His eventual victory was total and lasting. The symbolism of Jesus' life shows us that eternal life and continuous living service to God and humanity are the enduring rewards for those who live a life of dedication and dare to be themselves.

One of the greatest rewards of my work is to have the privilege and inspiration of living and working with completely dedicated people—those who have found the meaning of life and ask nothing else except the privilege of serving the ideals in which they believe. No work is too hard, no task too menial, no hours too long for such people. I was always inspired by a man in Santa Barbara who gave generously and worked faithfully in the service of the Church of Religious Science there. Whenever we tried to thank him he would say, "I should thank you. It is my pleasure to give. It is my privilege to serve."

The dedication and self-sacrifice of my wife, Bernice, was a good example of a completely purposeful life. While she was enjoying a successful business career of her own, she became a student of the late Emmet Fox. The inspired teachings of this great teacher helped her get her personal problems straightened out; from then on, she became an earnest student of Truth. Continuing her business career with great success, she also enrolled in Dr. Raymond Barker's classes in New York. This is where we met, and were married not long afterward.

Bernice immediately abandoned her own pursuits and dedicated herself to helping me follow the call of my teaching work. Bernice handled all the details during the early days as we travelled back and forth from New York to Philadelphia, Atlantic City, and other cities in the East, to present my lectures and classes. The endless details of arrangements, accommodations, bookkeeping, volunteer personnel, literature distribution, advertising and publicity, mailing, television and radio appearances, were all handled by Bernice.

From an active and independent life of her own, she assumed a role requiring her to remain in the background, and created the setting for me to lecture and teach. She was perfectly willing for me to receive the recognition and reap the glory. She preferred to do her work quietly, on the inner planes of life, without outer recognition of any kind. A dedicated servant to humanity, Bernice at the same time knew the importance of practicality in dealing with the everyday things of life.

True dedication entails the recognition and the unification of ourselves with a purpose, goal or idea which is greater than we are. To develop our magnificent potential, we must break through the tyranny of the little personality—the false ego—and let the imprisoned splendor come through.

The premise of this chapter is that one must be a *dedicated* person before one can be an *effective one*. The attitude of dedication must be basic in our approach to life before we can achieve lasting happiness, health or prosperity. I certainly do not want to give the impression that everyone should follow my path and become a teacher and minister. Perhaps some of you will—you are greatly needed—but most of you who are reading this book will apply these principles to your own fields of endeavor so that you may reach your true potential. This magnificent potential emerges when your life is motivated by purpose, meaning and a true desire to serve. The result is dedication, one of the basic inner attitudes which automatically produce a richer, fuller life.

Dedication does not imply suffering, struggle or lack—quite the opposite. Every one of us is knowingly or unknowingly dedicated to something. The successful person is the one who consciously chooses that to which he is to be dedicated. Dedication is the process by which we eliminate the evil, the false and the ugly from our consciousness, and pledge ourselves to follow the good, serve the true, and worship the beautiful. We don't even begin to glimpse our true potential until we are dedicated to something bigger than ourselves.

There was once a troublesome and hypochondriacal patient of generous proportions who continued to pester her doctor, begging for therapy and prescriptions, though there was no apparent need for them.

One day, after one of many unnecessary visits from this patient, the doctor wrote out this prescription: "Take one trip to Niagara Falls."

"Niagara Falls!" exclaimed the patient, "Why on earth should I go to Niagara Falls?"

"Because," replied the doctor, "I just want you to get a look at something bigger than yourself."

This is a hard lesson to come by for some of us, but it is my belief that this book will make the way somewhat easier for you. Let's start right here and now by dedicating ourselves to a life of purpose, meaning and service. Once we take this big step, everything else in our lives will fall into place.

A man I shall call Joe Smith took the step. Today his happy, purposeful and successful life is evidence of the fact that something happens when we get ourselves out of the way and let something bigger come through. This is his story.

The Joe Smith Story

Joe Smith is an everyday person living in a small Eastern city. He could be any one of us.

Joe stood in front of my desk late one afternoon, a belligerent scowl on his face as he twisted his soiled deliveryman's cap in his hands, and exploded: "I don't even know why I'm here—and I wouldn't be if I could have made my delivery truck go any place else this afternoon. This is the fifth time I have passed your church since lunch. Maybe you can tell me what gives."

"Perhaps I can, if you will give me a little more to go on," I replied.

"Well it's just this, Dr. Curtis. I know a little something about your teaching of the Science of Mind—at least I have heard you on the radio. I've always intended to come to your church, but I have never gotten around to it."

"You have plenty of company there," I smiled.

"Oh, I've wanted to, but I thought I would like to talk to you alone first. I want to find out more about this Science of Mind. I have a hunch it's something I would like to have my kids learn about. Then maybe they could avoid some of the mistakes I have made."

"Well, we're geared for the whole family," I said. "We'd be happy to have your children in our junior church—but let's talk about you for a minute. What about these mistakes you have made—and exactly what is troubling you today?"

As it turned out, several things were bothering Joe. No single one of them too important, but together they added up to a state of mind that he described as "like having a rock in my shoe." Something was always bothering him, he was dissatisfied and unhappy, he didn't feel as if he were getting any place, and his marriage was tottering.

Joe told me that he came from a typical middle-class American family. He had left college sometime before World War II to go to work as a salesman, for one simple reason—to make money. He became moderately successful by using high-pressure and personally aggressive methods. He worked hard, and pushed himself with the objective of getting ahead as fast as possible. His attitude toward life and business and his work habits placed a considerable strain upon his marriage, and he found little satisfaction in the success he had achieved. In his own words: "I didn't really think about anything but myself and what I wanted. Everything I was doing was by personal will-power alone. I had a good deal of anxiety, I was short-tempered and irritable, and I actually wasn't getting much out of life."

Of his Army experience which followed shortly after, Joe said: "Oh, I got ahead all right, but I never thought about anyone but myself. I didn't care who I stepped on."

After the war, Joe went back into his sales work in the East. But even though he was successful, his ambition and drive created so much pressure that to save his marriage he left the sales work which he loved so much, and moved from New York to a smaller city nearby. There he took a job driving a delivery truck on a commission basis. His natural ability soon brought him a supervisor's job, but as he said:

"The work was no challenge to me, and I felt as if I were wasting my life. I wasn't interested in my customers or the people with whom I worked. My approach was still that of a top sergeant, and my disposition was terrible. I was dissatisfied and disgusted with myself, so I took it out on others."

In addition, a factor of dishonesty had crept into Joe's life which disgusted him even more. This is the confession which he made to me that first afternoon he found his way into my office:

"I might as well tell you the truth. I have figured out ways to drag down more profit than my ordinary percentage on the delivery route by overcharging, falsifying records, "forgetting" to record certain sales, and things like that. I have protected myself in such a way that it will always look like a mistake—but I'm not kidding myself. I'm a thief—not much of a one, but a thief. And I'll tell you the truth, Dr. Curtis, I hate myself for it. I want your help. Nothing else is going right either—my wife is just about fed up again, I owe everybody in town, and I feel lousy most of the time. I'm about to blow my top."

I decided that afternoon that Joe Smith was willing to change himself in order to change his life for the better.

We decided that the following factors were behind Joe's problems: One, Joe wasn't doing the kind of work he liked or was best fitted for; two, he had a wrong idea of success; three, he was selfish, never really thinking of anything or anyone but himself; four, he had no purpose in life, no faith, and no real confidence in himself.

What did we do about it? The first step was to dissolve the false ideas and attitudes by adopting the opposite. We went right down the line in Joe's mind, and when there was a negative or destructive pattern, we used affirmative prayer to establish a constructive one.

He left our first meeting calm and serene, and with a new resolve in his face. The scowl was gone, and the cocky, quarrelsome personality was almost magically changed into one that was kind, considerate and likable. This was only the beginning. The Silent Partner took it from there. All Joe Smith and I did from there on in our subsequent meetings was to remind ourselves in prayer of those truths which had been uncovered for us the first time we had talked.

Joe Smith became a leader in his community. He again became a successful salesman, high up in the national ratings of his company. He was active in the work of his local Religious Science Church and never tired of giving his time, his attention and his support to the people and projects, so that this scientific teaching of an affirmative way of life could be brought to everyone the world over. He, his wife, and their son and daughter worked along with millions of others to make these ideas the means by which all of us may find our way into richer, fuller living.

Joe became sold on an idea, and then dedicated himself to it. Results naturally followed. This has been true in my life and it will be in yours when you start to use the Master Key to Success: *Find out what you have to give and then give it with all your heart, mind, soul and strength.* This is true dedication. This gives meaning and purpose to your life. This releases your true potential and brings to you whatever is necessary for an abundant life. I'm sure this is what Jesus was talking about when he instructed: "Seek ye first the kingdom of God, and His righteousness; and all these things shall be added unto you."

Although we live in a civilization where material things are important, they should be considered in their proper relationship to the real issues of life, not as ends in themselves. When we are truly dedicated to living the full life we will ask, "What can I give life?" rather than, "What can I get out of it?" Once we learn the habit of giving, the getting will take care of itself.

In the complex business affairs of a large church organization, for example, we are constantly confronted with cold, hard material facts. Rents, salaries and other expenses must be paid; we must balance outgo with income. This is the natural economic order. The income in a spiritual organization must come through the free-will sharing of those who depend upon the organization for their spiritual food. Whenever a shortage occurs or pressure arises, the situation quickly rights itself when we re-examine our motives, re-dedicate ourselves to giving, and renew our efforts to serve.

What is true of an organization is certainly true of an individual. If you are having trouble with the facts of existence, focus your attention upon the realities of dedication, sharing, and service, and the problem will be healed at the level of its cause—your own consciousness.

All organizations pledged to the service of God and humanity depend upon the many dedicated people serving them to carry on their work. These loyal people do what they are doing because they believe in it. Their dedication is often their only reward, and they know there is none greater.

The many teachers, ministers and practitioners in the Religious Science movement are dedicated servers, bringing the message of constructive thinking and the practical application of spiritual laws to many thousands of people throughout the world. This work has all stemmed from the dedication of one man, Dr. Ernest Holmes, who started the Institute of Religious Science and Philosophy in Los Angeles many years ago.

As a noted teacher, lecturer and writer, and as publisher of the Science of Mind Magazine, Dr. Holmes inspired many with his philosophy of richer, fuller living. Thousands of students were trained in his classes. They came from all walks of life, and soon many successful business and professional men were abandoning their careers to go out and start churches of their own, dedicating their lives to bringing this teaching to others. In a comparatively short time, the Religious Science movement has grown to include hundreds of churches. Even though it is not yet large in the eyes of the world, Religious Science provides a vital spiritual impetus and is performing a dedicated service to mankind.

Dr. Holmes believed that the Religious Science movement was the important idea for the age, and he dedicated himself completely to bringing it about. He believed that the movement should be organized if it were to endure. Therefore he built a central headquarters in Los Angeles, with a course of study which set high standards for leaders and practitioners. The new multimillion-dollar sanctuary was completed just a few months before Dr. Holmes died in April 1960. The seeds which he planted will continue to bear fruit for a long time to come.

Whatever success I myself have had in this field began many years ago when I sat high in a balcony seat in a large theatre in Los Angeles to hear Dr. Ernest Holmes speak. At that time he was in the prime of his public work. Even without understanding his teaching at first, I knew that the man had something. It was what he *was* that captivated me. His dedication, purpose and inner vision shone through to me constantly.

Years later, Dr. Holmes became one of my closest friends and advisors. For several years I spent extended periods as a guest in his home. Our regular evening discussions about the deep spiritual issues of life and their application to our experience have provided me with a priceless heritage. True, we did not always agree on certain points, but that was not important. The important thing was to come alive with insight and dedication and to go on from there.

Dr. Ernest Holmes inspired many of us who today are practitioners, teachers and leaders in just this way. He never tried to tell anyone how or what to think. He never imposed his ideas upon anyone, but he had a unique gift of inspiring people to catch fire with their own individuality. He discouraged everyone from trying to be like him, or even from trying to follow him. He simply used to say: "You know, the basis of this thing we are talking about is very simple, but it works. Now, you understand just as much about it as I do. I express it in my way; you must express it in yours—but come on, let's all work together in the same direction, so our vision has a chance to get somewhere."

Dr. Holmes gradually made Science of Mind a household word through his magazine, and through books, study courses, and radio and television broadcasts in which he carried his philosophy to millions of people.

But the teaching has spread not so much through those of us who teach it as through those who live it. The Science of Mind is a practical philosophy of life, and it works. In addition to those who follow the Science of Mind through the Religious Science churches and the other New Thought churches and centers, this philosophy has spread to many in the more established religious groups, and has certainly brought a more practical and affirmative approach to all spiritual thought. Dr. Ernest Holmes, a little man with a big heart and a big idea, certainly succeeded in waking up a lot of people and getting our lives turned in the right direction.

I, for one, am deeply grateful for the heritage which Dr. Holmes left. May his dedication continue to live on in the hearts of all people.

There are dedicated servers in every walk of life. People must recognize where they can *best* serve, and not try to be everything to all people. Unintelligent activity robs us of our purpose and our energy and renders us ineffective. Discrimination and judgment must be used on the high road of dedicated service, just as in everyday affairs. We constantly walk the razor's edge between the true and the false, between the vital and the trivial, and between the important and the unnecessary. It takes dedication to spiritual development to be able to tell the difference.

My own spiritual odyssey has taken me to the feet of many dedicated teachers. My quest started with the broad basic teaching of the Science of Mind, as I have related, and this has provided a solid foundation for me, just as it has for the thousands whom I have been privileged to teach. Basic Science of Mind is the starting point, but there is no limit to the expansion of our understanding, because we are exploring the realms of inner space, which are infinite.

I have crossed the country many times, just to see and study with a certain teacher. Even today, in the midst of my busy schedule, I often attend classes of other teachers, constantly reaching out to know more; yet at the same time reaching inward through prayer and meditation for the same purpose. In the remaining chapters of this book we shall center our discussion on practical techniques of personal growth and demonstration of specific results, but in this present chapter I wish to awaken you to the joys and rewards of the spiritual quest. To discover and live constantly in the awareness of God-indwelling is the most sublime adventure that life has to offer. Come along and discover it for yourself!

DAILY GUIDE TO DEDICATION

Today I dedicate myself to the larger life. I know who I am, why I am here and where I am going. I dedicate my life to the service of God and humanity. I dedicate myself to noble thoughts, words and deeds. I do good whenever and wherever I can. I give myself freely for the good of all. I dedicate myself to a larger purpose, I grow to become my real self. I am not concerned with what I can get out of life. I think only of what I can give. The Universal Creative Law balances all things, and I have whatever I need whenever I need it. I express a larger purpose in my life today.

I dedicate myself to quality rather than quantity. I am interested in "how good" rather than "how much." I dedicate myself to being my true self to the best of my ability at all times. I know that I am here on earth for a purpose and I do my very best to discover and fulfill that purpose. I am here to live, to learn, and to grow. I am joyously alive! I embrace every experience—good or bad—as a step forward in my development. I give life everything I have and it is returned to me a thousandfold. I dedicate myself to discovering and expressing the riches of the kingdom within me. To the best of my ability I dedicate myself to being a perfect human being. I am on fire with the will to live.

I say, "Father, use me." I dedicate myself to doing that which is for the greatest good of the greatest number. I am my brother's keeper and I do for him whatever I can. I carry my load in the world. I do my job. I accept my responsibilities and I discharge them to the best of my ability. I dedicate myself to noble goals, ideals and purposes. I avoid all trivial and second-rate activities. I always choose the upward path. I resist all temptation to be less than myself. I dedicate myself to the good, the true and the beautiful. I am true to myself and I cannot then be false to anyone. I dedicate my entire life to becoming perfect even as my Father in heaven is perfect. And so it is.

Hitch Your Wagon to a Star

What is your objective? What do you intend to do about it? How are you working toward it? Are you utilizing your inner potential to achieve results? Here are four steps that can help you to do so:

HOW TO ACCOMPLISH YOUR OBJECTIVE

1. Get clearly in mind what you want.
2. Develop a strong conviction that it is already yours.
3. Do everything you can to bring it about.
4. Release it, forget about it, go on about your business and let it happen. Sustain your conviction by giving thanks that it is already done.

This magic formula for accomplishment first came to my attention one evening many years ago when the Science of Mind Men's Club in our Santa Barbara church was discussing "Success and How to Achieve It." Many worthwhile suggestions were given, but the discussion never really got anywhere until a quiet, distinguished, grey-haired man spoke up and enumerated the above four points as his way of achieving success. He had come in late and none of us knew him, yet from the moment he spoke, he became the center of the discussion. He carried an air of unmistakable authority; his soft voice and considerate manner, plus the simplicity, clarity and logic of the four steps, made a deep impression on everyone.

Immediately we all started to put the steps into practice, and many of us achieved remarkable results. There are many similar success formulas, of course, but I have never found one with the impact of this one. I have taught it in every class I have given since, used it on countless radio and TV broadcasts, and always check myself out with it in anything I want to accomplish. This simple formula always works. I have seen its results in the lives of hundreds of men and women whom I have counseled personally. Its effectiveness lies in its very simplicity. It covers the main points of the creative process, and can be summarized as follows:

1. Get clearly in mind .... Thinking Step .... Thought
2. Develop a strong conviction .... Responding Step .... Feeling
3. Do everything you can .... Working Step .... Action
4. Forget it and let it happen .... Releasing Step .... Acceptance

Properly understood and practiced, these steps can be worth a million dollars to anyone who uses them. They were to Dr. Fernley H. Banbury, the quiet gentleman I mentioned above, who first gave me this technique. Dr. Banbury and I later became good friends, and he was quite active in our church in Santa Barbara. However, it was a long time before I learned who he really was. Fernley H. Banbury was widely known in the tire industry as the inventor of the Banbury Mixer, a device for mixing or incorporating pigments into the crude rubber compound essential in the manufacture of rubber tires. This invention made him an important figure in business for many years. Dr. Banbury himself was ample proof that his own simple system of thought and action works.

Getting Clearly in Mind What You Want

"What salary do you expect on this job?" a personnel manager asked a young woman of my acquaintance many years ago. She was reporting for her final interview before starting work. Having already passed the aptitude tests, the young woman was considered the ideal applicant for the job.

"Well—er—I don't exactly know," she stammered. "Uh—would $350 a month be too much?" (Salaries were much lower then.)

"$350!" the personnel man exclaimed. "Well, hardly! We had expected to pay at least $400 for an important position like this. I'm sorry, Miss Brown. If you don't put any more value than that upon your abilities, I'm afraid you're not what we are looking for. If you had asked for, say, $425 you would have had the job. Good day, Miss Brown. Better luck next time."

Miss Brown sobbed heartbrokenly as she told me her story. She had found exactly the job she wanted and now she had lost it because of two factors: she had not formed a clear and complete picture of what she wanted, and she lacked confidence in her own worth. She had failed to prepare herself consciously for her big opportunity, and so she lost it.

This happens all the time because people fail to realize the importance of forming a clear mental image of their desired objective. I explained this to Miss Brown, and together we discussed the type of job she wanted. We discussed her abilities, her training, and her plans for the future, and finally there emerged a clear picture of the job she wanted.

We went on to describe it in detail, fixing it firmly in mind until she could actually see the job and see herself in it. I also explained to her that the function of her conscious, or thinking mind was to initiate the action by choosing exactly what she wanted. This action gets under way when we declare our *intention* of achieving a particular good. There is no point in wishing or hoping or wanting or desiring something if we do not *intend* to achieve it. Clarity of choice and strength of intention go hand in hand. *Intend* to succeed and you will succeed.

Remember that to achieve anything worthwhile you must know

clearly what you want, you must *really* want it, and you must *intend* to get it.

Miss Brown understood this, even though she continued to mourn the loss of the job she had failed to land.

"Forget it," I counseled. "Let go of past mistakes, prepare your mind to create the image of what you want, and stand by for action. There is no lack of jobs, or anything else, for people who know what they want, intend to get it, and are prepared to receive it. Now let's go to work."

Together we worked out the following affirmation:

"I am in my right place, doing my right job. I know that the one right job wants me as much as I want it. I am the one right person for this job. I accept a position commensurate with my ability, my training, my experience and my potential for advancement. I am now employed by the right company, under the proper arrangements, with favorable working conditions, and at a salary which represents my true worth and meets my every need. I accept this job now, or its equivalent or better. I give thanks that this is so. And so it is."

Miss Brown definitely received "the equivalent or better." She found a fine position at a higher salary than any she had previously received, and with ideal conditions and opportunity for advancement. After a few months on the job she met one of the executives of the company, and they were married shortly afterward. All this would never have happened if Miss Brown had not developed her intention to live up to her full potential.

My files are filled with similar stories of men and women who are experiencing richer, fuller lives as the result of learning how to use the power within them. It can happen to you. The simple steps of this book will put you in contact with your own magnificent potential.

How to Choose Your Goal Wisely

In this book we are interested in opening up the vistas of a larger life for everyone. We are working with a tremendous power, however, and it must be used wisely. If we are to attain our full potential, we must raise our sights above mere whims and selfish desires. We are aiming higher than getting things just because we think we want them. Wisdom, judgment and understanding are necessary prerequisites for maturity.

We must also learn to align our wants and our needs. We had better do so, for what we need is always what we get. Now, when you do want something, ask yourself a few simple questions: "Is this what I need? Does this help me express what I really am? Is this the right thing at this time? Will this hurt anyone? Will the fulfillment of this desire of mine contribute to the general good? Is this right action? Is this for the best interests of everyone concerned?"

If you can answer all of these questions favorably, then it's full steam ahead. Go to it—get the creative process under way. Work thoroughly upon the four steps, starting by getting your goal clearly in mind and sharpening your intention to achieve it. Then coordinate all of your creative powers to bring it about.

Remember, you would not have had this idea or desire unless you were supposed to do something about it. It is for you to decide what. The decision is yours. Obviously, you will decide more wisely if you have firmly prepared yourself by developing the first five steps on our Ladder of Accomplishment—Relaxation, Expectation, Recognition, Unification and Dedication.

Many people, however, are blocked in the reaching of their objectives because of superstition about, and ignorance of, the working of the Creative Law. "I don't know if God wants me to have this," they say. "I don't know if this is good for me. How am I to know if it is God's will?"

Superstitious questions such as these can only grow out of personal indecision. There is no arbitrary or self-conscious God keeping track of what we should or should not have. We have been given the power of choice plus the power of judgment. It is up to us to use them. God can work *for* us only by working *through* us.

A method of being sure you are on the right track is to measure the worth of your desire or objective according to the standards we have indicated. If it adds up to good, God wants you to have it. The will of good is the will of God. You are expressing God's will when you raise your mature spiritual judgment to the level of conviction. Intention itself is then a vital step in the process of demonstrating a specific good. God's will is the will of life. This is the only will there is. Anything less is blockage and limitation. Be clear in your intention and you will be in tune with life.

The Will to Win

The desire to succeed is standard equipment for any normal human being. Evolution is the law of life, and evolution means growth. Growth means change, and change means adjustment. Happy people are well adjusted to life. Successful people add a measure of personal accomplishment to this adjustment. And people who are happy and successful always intend to do something with their lives. They are constantly moving toward the top. Their best efforts are directed to assist the processes of growth, improvement and accomplishment. They have the will to win. They *intend* to succeed.

The late Dr. Robert A. Millikan, a famous physicist, realized at the beginning of his career that he needed to be free from all financial worries and pressures if he were to be successful in the program of research to which he wished to devote his life. He intended to accomplish his objectives, so his affirmation was: "I have a lavish and dependable income consistent with integrity and mutual benefits." The creative power of the subconscious mind had no trouble getting the message of an intention so clearly expressed. Dr. Millikan not only accomplished his professional goals, but he also demonstrated everything he needed in life in the process. Everything unfolded from his intention to succeed.

On the other hand, many people have a subconscious desire to fail. Psychologists have pointed out many reasons for this: a deep sense of inferiority and inadequacy, a desire to punish oneself or others, a bid for pity and attention, an unwillingness to assume responsibility, an inability to face life. If you are caught in a failure pattern, check your inner intention and ask yourself honestly and bluntly: "Did I intend to succeed or fail?" The answer may surprise you.

Remember, we always experience the sum total of our inner attitudes of mind. Probe deeply enough and you will find the cause behind every experience. Success or failure, health or sickness, happiness or unhappiness, abundance or limitation, are all effects of our inner states of mind.

Which do you choose? What kind of life do you intend to have? Decide what you want, meet the requirements spiritually, mentally, emotionally, and actively, and go ahead and get it. There is nothing stopping you. Develop your intention to succeed now.

Over the years, I have had the privilege of helping thousands of men and women in their quest for richer, fuller lives. We always start by getting their thinking straightened out, overcoming their feelings of inadequacy, and getting them to believe that they can be and do better than they thought they could. This sometimes takes some doing. The will to fail, fed by fear, inferiority and doubt, is actually the will to succeed—at being a failure! When personally counseling these people I always close each discussion with a period of scientific prayer treatment. All negative ideas, thoughts and attitudes are thus systematically dissolved, and attitudes of constructive intention are established in the mind. This can be accomplished during a session or two, but it often takes longer, because the inner negative fear and failure patterns have deep roots which have been established over a long period of time.

For instance, one young man came to me for counseling and treatment regarding a new job he was after. I ended my treatment with strong statements of affirmation for the purpose of building up constructive attitudes of mind and developing a positive intention of success.

We completed the treatment with the statement: "I accept this job, its equivalent or better." However, I had hardly stopped speaking before the young man said, "But I know I'll never get it; there's too much competition. I don't have any pull with those big shots, and besides, I don't think I've had enough training and experience. . . ."

"Just a minute," I interrupted. "Do you want this job or not?"

"Why, of course I do," he flared. "Why do you think I am here?"

"Then why are you ruining everything we've been doing for the past hour?" I asked.

"What do you mean?"

"Listen to yourself. You had half a dozen negative statements ready before I had even finished praying."

"Well, I don't know, Dr. Curtis. Things are awfully tough."

"Do you want to keep on thinking things are tough or do you want to get that job and make a success of things?"

What my young friend was doing, of course, was using his priceless inner imaging faculty to picture the worst of everything. William James said, "When there is a conflict between the will and the imagination, the imagination always wins." I explained this, and we started over again. Slowly but surely, over a period of a few weeks, as we worked together with the twelve constructive steps on our Ladder of Accomplishment, the young man's outlook changed; his failure pattern was transferred into an intention to succeed.

In time, he found that the original job he had thought he wanted so much was not the one for him at all. During the course of our counselling and treatment sessions, we discovered the reason for his failures and negative outlook. He was only trying to make a go of it in business because of parental insistence. He really wanted to be a motion picture actor. He never intended to succeed in any other kind of work. Subconsciously he intended to fail even while he was consciously trying, as he thought, to succeed. This naturally led to an inner conflict which made any progress in either direction impossible. All of this came out during our sessions together. Now, I never advise a person what he should do. This decision rests solely with the person involved. But I do point out that the decision must be made. The intention must be clear or progress is impossible. It is better for a person to pursue a course of action which is right for him, no matter how difficult it may be, than to fritter away his life in halfhearted efforts in which he doesn't intend to succeed anyway.

In the case of my young friend, he made up his mind to follow his star into the motion picture industry, even after my detailed explanation of the problems and pitfalls involved.

We sharpened his intention with the following affirmation: "I am constantly, continually, constructively, creatively and profitably employed in the television and motion picture industry as an actor with roles, salary and arrangements commensurate with my ability, my potential and my will to succeed."

My friend built a solid reputation as a good actor. His progress was steady from the beginning. He was a dedicated student of the

Science of Mind. At the same time he used its principles to help him succeed, and he helped others do the same. This is the way the idea spreads, and I am glad to say that more and more people are finding their way into rich and meaningful lives every day through the application of these principles.

This teaching is the hope of the world. All we have to do is use it. The principles are as old as time—all the idealistic philosophers and great spiritual leaders have taught them. It just remains for all of us to put them to work in our own lives, remembering with Jesus, "And, if I be lifted up from the earth, I will draw all men into me."

Moreover, as we rise above our problems and difficulties we make it easier for the next person. There is absolutely no need to fritter away our lives in aimlessness, despair, illness, fear or limitation. Follow your star. Really intend to make its brilliance your own. We become great by keeping eternally at it.

DAILY GUIDE TO INTENTION

Today I intend to live life fully. I intend to be my best and to do my best at all times. I know that I am here in this life to grow mentally, emotionally and spiritually. Today I am building more stately mansions in my soul. I have the best intentions at all times. My motives are pure and my intentions to be a better person are strong and true. I eliminate all unworthy thoughts and feelings from my consciousness. I am in control of what I think, say, feel and do. I am emotionally mature, mentally alert, and spiritually attuned. I do a good job of this business of living.

Today I align myself with worthy objectives. I have no time for second-rate interests or activities. I work out a sensible plan for my life and I intend to carry it out. I take inventory of my character today, and eliminate all unworthy traits. I intend to be true to myself and I know that I cannot then be false to any man. I learn to live, I learn to love, I learn to know. I know that there is a perfect idea of me in the mind of God, and I intend to achieve that perfection. I intend to be physically strong, mentally awake and morally straight. I learn to understand humanity. I intend to love my neighbor as myself and to live by the Golden Rule at all times. I offer myself freely wherever help is needed. I love to serve and I serve wisely and well.

Whatever my hand finds to do, I do it with all my might, "as unto the Lord and not unto men." I know there is more to life than meets the eye, and I intend to find out what it is. I intend to be in my right place at the right time and to fully live up to what is expected of me. I do my very best to make other people happy and to be happy myself. I intend to live up to every high intention I set for myself. I must be about my Father's business at all times. I intend to live so that my life may be taken as a model for all people. I intend to be a good person today and always. And so it is.

8

❖ ❖ ❖

God Cannot Say No

You will recall the description in Chapter 3 of my wife's dream of her ideal house, the treatments we gave for it, and the events leading up to finding the wonderful site for it in Santa Barbara. Remember that we *expected* to find just the right spot upon which to build. I am continuing that story here because it demonstrates so perfectly the unfolding of our twelve steps, and that what we experience in life is inevitably the result of our inner beliefs and attitudes. Now, I don't want to give the impression that we spent all of our time praying for this house. Our home was to be just part of the total picture of the life which we were endeavoring to build—a life that would fully express the philosophy we were teaching.

Right from the beginning, we *intended* to have such a life. We *intended* to have such a home. And, as the creative process unfolded, we assisted it fully by *identifying* ourselves with it. When you identify yourself with something you actually *become* that thing, and it becomes you. The importance of this step in the creative process cannot be overstated. There must be complete identification or there can be no complete demonstration of the result.

In searching for the site of our home, Bernice and I had identified ourselves completely with the objectives which we desired—beauty, peace, and seclusion in a natural setting of mountains, space and sea. We had always subconsciously embodied this picture, but we had only started to state it consciously at the time established in Chapter

3. The ensuing years of constant thought, discussion and treatment were building this identification.

We had started with an idea, but no money. However, with the income from my acting assignment in *The Ten Commandments*, we were able to purchase our "dream site." But after buying the land, we had no money left with which to build our house, so we bided our time, going about our busy lives, doing regular treatment upon the situation, and playing the game of identification by visualizing our house as *already built.*

Whenever we could we spent time at our mountain wonderland, drinking in the beauty, and breathing in its atmosphere. We actually marked off an imaginary kitchen and ate our picnic lunches there. Then we placed our chairs and feasted in our imaginary dining room. In the same way we meditated before our "fireplace" and read in our "library." I wrote and studied in my "den," our car was parked in the "garage," and we had sunbaths as we stretched out on the pads in our "bedroom." We carefully marked off the foundation of the house and outlined the patio. We set out trees and plants, and we dreamed of that which was already real to us. This was total identification.

And it worked. Our affairs prospered during the year and there was an appreciation in the value of our property sufficient to enable us to obtain a building loan. Within a few more months our dream house actually stood in the place where we had built castles in the air.

The day we moved in, Bernice was preparing dinner in our model kitchen with its picture window looking out on majestic La Cumbre Peak. Suddenly she called, "Darling, come here—quickly!"

"What is it?" I asked anxiously.

"Look—it's my road!"

"Your road—what road?" I questioned.

"Ours—winding up the hill. Isn't that strange. It's my road—only it's turned the other way."

"What road turned the other way when?" I asked, mystified.

It seemed that Bernice had had a recurring dream since childhood in which she had seen a winding road leading up a hill. When she looked out at our road she realized that her dream had materialized exactly—except that the road curved in the opposite direction. I pointed out that this would of course be true, since the *outer* road was the reverse of the *inner* road of the dream—just as a picture appears upside down in the lens of a camera.

It was indeed a remarkable experience—and graphic evidence of the creative power of the mind. We are always learning such lessons from our personal experiences and from the lives of those we are privileged to help.

The Bill Brown Story

A young man whom I shall call Bill Brown provided one such lesson. When I first met Bill, he was out of work for the first time in his life. He was only in his early forties, but he had had a remarkable career. His background included everything from rum-running during prohibition to radio announcing, which had been his last job.

How did Bill come to be unemployed at this period of his life, which is for most men the period when they are just entering the most productive time of their careers? This will take a little answering.

Bill had been born into meager circumstances. Things were not too happy between his parents, and life for Bill became a bleak, dreary existence, a constant struggle to make ends meet. There never seemed to be enough of anything to go around, and an atmosphere of defeat, poverty and failure surrounded the home. The boy rebelled against it, and very early in his life he started to make his own way. Working and saving, he was able to have many things he wanted, even though the rest of the family had to fend for themselves. A pattern of self-centeredness became firmly entrenched in Bill early in his life.

Bill wasn't really personally ambitious; he just wanted enough money to feel secure. As a young man, he settled on the largest amount he could conceive of—$10,000. At that time, this seemed like all the money in the world. Nevertheless, this remained his figure, and he bent all his efforts toward saving that much.

Let me say right here that Bill was not a bad man—there is nothing wrong with desiring security, and saving money. It is necessary and right that we do this; however, there is a right and a wrong way of going about it.

In Bill's case, going about it included many activities and jobs, some legitimate and some not. He would do anything for money; $10,000 was his goal and that was the only thing that mattered. At a time when many young men are finishing high school and going on to college, Bill had long since left his parents' home and was working at whatever came his way. Instead of learning a trade or a profession, he skipped the tedium and study of apprenticeship, turned down many offers, and concentrated on the "easy money."

Eventually, Bill did make his $10,000. When that happened, he felt he had all of the security that he would ever need. He and his wife lived simply; Bill obtained a job as radio announcer for a small station at a salary far below any he had ever worked for, just so he would have enough to pay expenses. Now he really didn't care about anything else; the security of his $10,000 was all he needed—so he thought.

But circumstances change. And suddenly they did with Bill. First, he developed a series of minor physical ailments through which he incurred heavy medical expenses. Then, too, the cost of living was going up, and he felt that he should be earning more money. He approached his employer for a raise, but even though his work was excellent, he was let go, and a younger man was hired at a lower salary.

Bill was bitter and resentful toward his former employer; he spent weeks in futile stewing and in plotting ways to get even, but not actually doing anything about it. When he did start to look for another job, his negative state of mind was so obvious to everyone that he couldn't find anything. Several months passed; with no income, Bill was forced to dip into the precious $10,000. This panicked him. Seeing his security vanishing, he desperately sought help.

Then he found it. He came to the Science of Mind Church and I was able to set him straight on many things. Bill saw that he simply had the creative life power within him running the wrong way. He had limited it by limiting himself. His goal was not worthy of him, so natural growth toward a better life was stifled. The energy within him had to go somewhere, so it worked destructively, first in his body, then in his job, and in his relationships with other people. His hate and resentment for the boss who fired him was a further step in the destructive process. Through the Science of Mind, this man was able to turn his thoughts around and get them running in constructive channels.

Bill's first step was forgiveness—starting with himself. Then he forgave the boss against whom he had harbored so much resentment; then on down the line he went, correcting within himself those attitudes which were working against him. During this process Bill Brown discovered things about himself that he had never known. New goals and new abilities came to light.

Bill found his niche in public service work where he had the opportunity to help many people each day; he became healthy and he is happy. The $10,000? I really don't know—but I do know that Bill Brown doesn't care, because he has discovered untold riches within his own heart—wealth that is coined in terms of inner peace and fulfillment.

VISUALIZATION—AND HOW IT WORKS

Perhaps the most valuable tool of the identification process is visualization—using the image-making faculty of the mind. When we learn to see in our "mind's eye," we provide the invisible pattern for the objects and experiences which will be projected into our world. To see is to know, to know is to be, and to be is to experience. *Keep ever before you the image of what you want to be.* Identify yourself in thought and visualize that which you have chosen. This may range all the way from getting a new pair of shoes to becoming a better person. What we see invisibly, tends to become visible; in fact, it always does when we sustain the image and have faith in its demonstration.

One man I knew, a large contractor and developer in Beverly Hills, used this same "picture principle" in setting up deals and laying out great housing projects and shopping centers. This man was also one of the leading members of the Science of Mind Church. We became very good friends, and discussed these matters many times. This very successful man never worried about how something was to be done. He concentrated on getting the picture of it clearly in mind. When the picture was clear, everything else followed in natural order.

This successful man told me that he worked mentally upon each picture as if it were a great mosaic. Every little piece must fit into its proper place. Only when this visualization process was completed and the entire image was fixed firmly in mind would he go ahead with his plans.

Visualization often leads to the development of the powers of intuition, inspiration and inner guidance. During World War II my contractor friend received an invitation from the Army to submit a quick bid along with one other contractor on a project involving several million dollars. Speed was of the essence and the bidders were given less than twenty-four hours to submit their bids, the lowest of which was to be awarded the contract. My friend and his staff worked all night going over specifications, costs and estimates, and dispatched their bid by messenger just under the deadline. However, in making a final check, my friend lowered one item by fifty cents before signing the bid.

"Ridiculous, wasn't it?" the contractor laughed in relating the story. "Imagine making a change of fifty cents in an estimate running into millions."

"Why did you do it?" I asked.

"Something just told me to," he relied. "I was ready to drop with exhaustion, but all of a sudden my mind became crystal clear and something said, 'Change it!' I did, and believe me I've always followed my hunches since."

"Did you get the job?" I asked.

"I'll say I did, and three others right after that were even bigger. And do you know the difference in those bids? Just fifty cents. If I hadn't made that final change we'd have had to flip a coin. The bids were identical except for that one item. You don't have to sell me on intuition. It works. Now go on and use it, Don—but be sure you see the picture!" He laughed as he went back to his desk.

Visualization has been my tool many times in working on specific personal needs and problems. Used properly, visualization can be a most valuable tool in identifying oneself with a particular good. Once, my wife and I found ourselves owing a large amount of money, and needing still more to carry out some of our plans. We decided to use visualization in working out the situation. First we made a neat pile of all of our current bills. It made quite a stack. Then we sat down at the desk together and as Bernice handed me each bill I stamped it with my fist and said, "Paid!" Then I placed it on a spindle.

We were using this method to impress upon the subconscious mind that the bills were paid. The principle is that *what you accept as true becomes true through the natural creative process.* This is the secret behind all successful prayer, treatment and demonstration.

To get back to the unpaid bills, let me make it clear that we were not engaging in magic, trickery, or delusion. We were merely going through a graphic visual discipline as one step toward our larger picture of expectation. It worked, as it always does. Don't ask me how, but within a short time—right on schedule—we found ourselves able to pay all our bills. There was a general upturn in our affairs, and I *earned* sufficient money to take care of all obligations. That is the way treatment works.

The Importance of Environment

Our outer surroundings are extremely important in the process of identification. We tend to become like the things we look upon or are in constant contact with. The beauty and the renewing forces of nature refresh us and keep us in balance. Our own mountain homesite in Santa Barbara had a profound and lasting effect upon Bernice and me because of its great peace and beauty. In this setting we became one with the mountains, the sea, the sky, the trees, the birds, and the animals.

As far as possible, see to it that your own surroundings and environmental contacts are compatible with what you want to be. Chameleon-like, we take on the qualities of our environment. To the best of your financial ability, wear good clothes, eat good food in good restaurants, stay in good hotels, drive a good car, and frequent those places where there is a harmonious, graceful and abundant consciousness. In the long run, it doesn't cost any more to have the best, and the lasting effect in identification will more than make up any difference.

The Science of Mind teaches a philosophy of abundance. Since all things proceed from the inner consciousness of the individual, we work to expand that consciousness. This, of course, is the purpose and the process of the twelve steps of this book. Life provides the best of everything. Identify yourself with it and it will become yours through perfectly natural means.

How to Use Visualization in Healing

The basis of our process of healing is to see the person whole and perfect. As practitioners we learn how to see through the apparent imperfection or difficulty and to focus upon the magnificent potential within the individual. If we are successful in sustaining this picture, the patient is healed.

Now, this process is not imagining or pretending; it is "seeing true"—looking through the outer factual appearance of effect to the inner reality of truth and cause. Jesus suggested that we are in the world, but not of it. He said "In the world ye shall have tribulation: but be of good cheer: I have overcome the world. . . . Judge not according to the appearance, but judge righteous judgment." Jesus believed, as Plato did, that there is a perfect pattern of all things in the Infinite Mind, and that this pattern, when not interfered with, will naturally project itself into outer manifestation. The same is true in healing; when we get rid of this interference, the natural wholeness—or health—is restored. This process entails the elimination of destructive mental and emotional attitudes, formation of new patterns of thought and reaction, and identification with the inner perfection which is present at the center of our being.

You can heal yourself right now by completely identifying yourself with health. No matter what the difficulty or the condition may be, focus your attention upon the inner perfection and creative power of God and say, "Where the problem seems to be, God is already there." See yourself doing those things which you can do in your normal, active, healthy state. Form a perfect image of your body and order your subconscious mind to produce it for you. If there has been a crippling disease or an accident, visualize the free movement of the affected part of your body. See yourself running, dancing, jumping and doing all of the things you would normally do. Anything you can do to identify yourself with wholeness and perfection will start the creative process working to bring it about.

Now I do not want to make any exaggerated claims, nor do I want anyone to be disappointed or disillusioned. I am presenting a principle. It is yours to use. I firmly believe that "with God all things are possible." I am also aware that we do not always get complete results; but we must keep trying. There are no "incurable" diseases. We are only limited by our lack of belief. Keep developing your faith, visualizing, and identifying yourself with the whole picture. Clearly embody the image of what you want to be. I have seen the sick healed, the lame walk, and the blind see. And in those cases where complete results are not achieved, there is always an improvement. When the individual identifies himself with the whole picture, he is either healed completely, or his attitude improves to such an extent that he is able to adapt himself to the situation and live a full life despite the handicap.

The world is full of men and women who have triumphed over difficulties by strengthening their inner attitudes toward life. The specific techniques and the affirmative steps developed in this book will accomplish worthwhile results for anyone who uses them.

Identify Yourself with Success

We become successful when we identify ourselves with success. You will never become a success if you identify yourself with failure. The inner image always reproduces itself in our experience.

Years ago, hopeful young actors like myself used to gather for coffee at a Times Square drugstore in New York. We would read the theatrical columns and discuss the current activities in the theatre; we would commiserate with each other about our inability to convince the casting offices that we were God's gift to the American theatre. At eleven o'clock, fortified by this atmosphere of gloom and defeat, we would start "making the rounds," trudging from office to office in search of employment. We would usually approach the receptionist with the timorous query: "You wouldn't have anything for me, would you?" or "I don't suppose there is any casting today, is there?"

The answer was invariably "no." We were licked before we started when we followed such a procedure. You can't get positive results from a negative attitude. You can't achieve anything when you believe you can't. The whining and begging actors never got the jobs. The ones who succeed in the highly competitive world of the theatre, or in anything else, are those who prepare themselves and develop their confidence in themselves and their ability. A persistent attitude that will not take "no" for an answer certainly gets more results than a talent that identifies itself with failure.

Hundreds of hopefuls, both young and old, used to come to me over the years asking: "How can I get into pictures—or the theatre, or TV?"

My answer was always, "You can't—unless you believe you can. There is no set way. You can do it if you have something on the ball, believe in yourself, and are willing to endure scorn, insults, rebuff, hardship and discouragement. If you want it enough, and if you can continue to see yourself up there with the stars no matter how tough it gets, you will make it. Otherwise, your heart will be broken. Now, do you still want it?"

The ones who are sufficiently identified with their dream will—and do—go through almost anything to get there. The rest fall by the wayside in the natural eliminative process of the survival of the fittest. I can name any number of stars and successful writers, directors and producers who slept on park benches, who washed dishes or worked as janitors, salesgirls or carhops on their way up the ladder. They finally got there because they were so completely identified with success that failure was impossible.

In my own career as an actor, I never needed to go quite that far, but I never got to the top either. In my youth I used to say, "If I can always have enough to eat, a place to sleep, and a part to play, I will be happy the rest of my life." It is obvious that I identified with an extremely limited goal. It took years to rise above it.

"You're sure you want to try this acting business?" my father questioned me one day during the depression years of the 1930s.

"Yes I do, Dad; that's all I want."

"Well, it's up to you. I don't know anything about it, but I want you to be sure you know what you're getting into. They tell me it is a pretty shaky business, and that most actors are out of work and broke most of the time. I had hoped you'd be a farmer, but since you don't like that, why don't you do something that's solid and has some security to it?"

"I'll make it, Dad. I know all about how tough it is, but that's what I want. I'm going to be an actor."

"All right, son. I guess you'll have to get it out of your system. But promise me one thing—that you'll finish your college education. Prepare yourself to make $200 a month so I won't have to worry about you."

So I stuck to my plan. I had already decided on the School of Speech at Northwestern University as the gateway to the magic world of the theatre. Two of my dramatic teachers had gone there and encouraged me to apply for a scholarship. When I got the promise of a partial scholarship and part-time work, I embarked on a day coach from Spokane to Chicago, with the blessing of my parents and their promise to help financially as much as they could. It worked out that my father helped me with part of my tuition for a couple of years, and everything else was up to me.

I worked at everything from dishwasher to crowd extra at the Chicago Civic Opera Company, and somehow I made it. They were tough years, but I was happy because I was identified with the theatre. I thought theatre, studied theatre, and acted and worked in the theatre all the time that I wasn't busy washing dishes, waiting on tables or doing janitor work. And I loved it.

When I wasn't involved at the School of Speech, I roamed Chicago, frequenting the theatres, working as an extra, an usher, or whatever I could to be near the magic world. I followed actors around like a puppy dog, practically worshiping them; I looked forward to the day when I could join their select company. I was the original stage-struck kid; I wouldn't take a million dollars for those wonderful years, but I wouldn't go through them again for the same amount.

When I arrived in Chicago on that daycoach, it was my first visit to a really big city. I had hayseeds in my hair and $25 in my pocket, but I had identified myself with a dream, and I knew I would make it. Still, I had my eye on much wider horizons. I wanted to get to New York. The magic word "Broadway" had beckoned to me for many years. So, though I didn't have a dime in my pocket, I decided to go to New York for Christmas to see the shows.

To earn money for the trip, I got a part-time job selling neckties during the Christmas season. I was a frightful salesman, but I stuck with it, hoping that I would make enough money to get to New York. Christmas was getting closer and I wasn't doing very well. My dream was fading, but somehow I knew I would make it. I did. A couple of days before Christmas, a whole mob of gangsters swept into the store to do their Christmas shopping. What did they want? Expensive neckties, of course. And who did the mob leader choose to buy them from? You guessed it. I guess I looked like I needed the business. Every salesman on the floor headed for the bonanza and started showing neckties, but the underworld chieftain waved them away. I was his man.

"Show me whatcha got, kid," he commanded.

"Here you are, sir," I stammered as I laid out some flashy models.

"Not that junk, punk! Show me something with some class— something real genteel. Don't worry about the price."

The gangsters ended up by cleaning the racks of every expensive tie in the place. Before it was over, the manager and every available salesman were called to my assistance. It was the biggest necktie sale in the history of the store.

Before the gang leader left, he told the manager: "I want all this stuff put on this kid's book, see? I'm his customer, and he gets credit for the sale. Merry Christmas!"

And he was gone in a cloud of expensive cologne and cigar smoke. I don't know which of the Chicago terrorists he was, but he served the purpose for me. After I had totaled up my earnings, I found that I had enough bonuses coming to buy my bus ticket, with nearly thirty dollars left over for my two weeks in New York. I was on my way! I quit my job right there, collected my pay, and got on a bus for New York.

It was all I had expected it to be. And what a time! Nine days of heaven! I was scared to death, but I was in New York, the most sophisticated city in the world. I endeavored to live up to its reputation. My derby hat, flowered muffler, too-short overcoat, cane, yellow gloves and tan shoes were my farm-boy's idea of what the best-dressed man should wear. I must have made an incongruous picture as I "did" New York.

I stayed in an unheated room in Greenwich Village but spent most of my time on Broadway. I managed to see seventeen plays in nine days—evenings, matinees, special performances—everything. Fifty cents a day was spent for food—no more—the rest went for theatre tickets.

I only stopped when I was flat broke—with only two days left to get back to school, a thousand miles away, and no money left to get there. I was mulling this over as I trudged along Times Square, when I ran into one of my professors from Northwestern. He was driving back to Chicago that day and asked me to come with him. Naturally I accepted.

Now, I am certainly not recommending any part of this youthful escapade of mine as the procedure to follow, but it is an excellent illustration of the power that surges through a person's life when his intention and identification join with his expectation. Neither am I asking you to believe that I did disciplined mental and spiritual treatment work upon the situation. I knew nothing about such things then. It was simply a matter of knowing what I wanted and getting it without recognizing any blockage or limitation.

A sound grasp of our twelve points will move you surely and steadily toward accomplishing *your* goals and purposes. Be definite in your intentions, pure in your motives, and complete in your identification. *Learn to control what you think and feel and you will control your experience.*

It was some years before I was to break through a number of limitations and become a successful actor. Even though I did everything possible to identify myself as one, I neglected to eliminate one very serious flaw in my thinking: *I didn't really believe I could make it.* My identification was faulty. I had the desire and the intention but I was never able to identify myself completely with the whole picture.

Consequently, my success as an actor was limited to the same extent that my identification was limited.

While my own experience was marked by many detours, all of them have since proved valuable. The first detour was my several years of experience as a college and university instructor immediately following my graduation. You remember that my father had urged me to prepare myself so that I could make $200 a month? Well, I did. My first college instructor's job paid exactly that; so did my second, and it was several years before I made any more than that. I had subconsciously identified myself with this figure and it took some time to rise above it. There had to be a change in my inner consciousness before it finally happened.

Our subconscious identification determines what we achieve. That is why we must constantly enlarge these subconscious patterns. Everything we think, say, feel, experience and believe forms the consciousness which conditions the subconscious mind. Identify yourself with the larger picture of what you intend to achieve. Accept no limitation. You *are* success. You *are* health. You *are* happiness. You *are* freedom. You *are* prosperity. You *are* order and right action. Identify yourself with these objectives and they are yours.

Having learned these principles, I experienced much less difficulty in identifying myself with my work as a teacher and minister. As soon as Dr. Barker's suggestion that I get into this work started to take hold of me, and I made my decision to enter this field, I started a process of conscious and subconscious identification which has never stopped and never will. Study, observation, experience, correction, learning by our mistakes, and constant clarification, through prayer and treatment are continuing steps in maintaining our identification with what we want to be.

We learn a great deal from those who have gone before us as well as from those who are presently working with us. Education and growth are never-ending experiences. Continuous study is essential. We have available to us all of the knowledge, wisdom and experience of the human race as it has been developed up to this time. Identify yourself with knowledge, wisdom and understanding. Read. Carry on conversations with the great minds of the past and the present. As we identify ourselves with them, their greatness becomes ours. Carry on conversations with God through prayer, treatment and meditation. As we identify ourselves with the Infinite Intelligence, we grow in nobility, effectiveness and power. Be what you are—a child of God. Live from the fullness of the great Presence within and your place in the world will take care of itself. *Identify* yourself with it, and it is yours.

A Program for Complete Identification

All things are created by God, the Infinite Intelligence, as we discussed thoroughly in the chapter on unification. Therefore we are one with the Source from which we come. So is the objective which we are endeavoring to manifest in our lives. This relationship is clearly indicated by the following diagram:

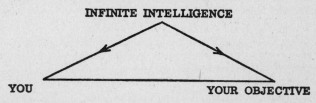

In completely identifying ourselves with our objectives we start by recognizing the flow of love between ourselves and the Infinite Intelligence. This is *unification*. Then we recognize this force of creative love flowing through us into our desired objective. This is *identification*. This visualizing process is indicated as follows:

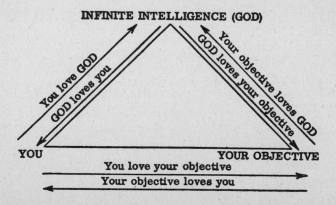

Fix this complete identification firmly in your mind by repeating such statements as these:

THERE IS ONE SOURCE FROM WHICH ALL THINGS FLOW.

THIS SOURCE IS IN ME AND I AM PART OF THIS INFINITE INTELLIGENCE.

I LOVE THIS SOURCE WHICH IS GOD.

GOD LOVES ME.

I AM ONE WITH GOD, THE INFINITE INTELLIGENCE, THE ONE SOURCE FROM WHICH ALL THINGS PROCEED.

THIS SOURCE IS IN MY DESIRED GOOD (NAME IT) AND MY DESIRED GOOD IS PART OF THIS INFINITE INTELLIGENCE.

MY OBJECTIVE (NAME IT) LOVES GOD.

GOD LOVES MY OBJECTIVE.

I LOVE MY OBJECTIVE.

MY OBJECTIVE LOVES ME.

GOD, MY OBJECTIVE AND MYSELF ARE ONE.

I AM COMPLETELY UNIFIED WITH GOD.

I AM COMPLETELY IDENTIFIED WITH MY OBJECTIVE.

GOD WANTS ME TO HAVE THAT WHICH IS GOOD FOR ME TO HAVE.

GOD CANNOT SAY NO.

GOD KNOWS WHAT THINGS I HAVE NEED OF BEFORE I ASK.

IT IS GOD'S GOOD PLEASURE TO GIVE ME THE KINGDOM.

I COOPERATE WITH THE CREATIVE ACTION WHICH IDENTIFIES ME COMPLETELY WITH MY DESIRED GOOD.

MY DESIRED GOOD WANTS ME AS MUCH AS I WANT IT.

I AM COMPLETELY IDENTIFIED WITH MY OBJECTIVE BY THE UNIVERSAL LAW OF ATTRACTION.

I MENTALLY ACCEPT MY OBJECTIVE AS BEING AN
ACTUAL FACT IN MY EXPERIENCE.
I AWAIT ITS MANIFESTATION WITH PERFECT CONFI-
DENCE.
IT IS DONE.
I GIVE THANKS THAT THIS IS SO.

Visually your complete identification with your desired good
looks like this:

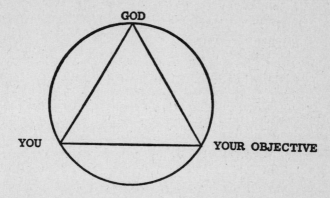

The circle represents completion. Keep this completed picture in
your mind and that with which you identify yourself in this way
must come about in your world.

Your Technique of Alignment

To be a whole person we must clearly identify ourselves with our
various "little selves" which go to make up the real Self that each
one of us is. There are seven of these "selves" which go to make up
the Whole Person:

1. *Environmental Self:* Outer expression, your world, experience, things, situations, problems, circumstances, conditions,
   actions, sense impressions.
2. *Physical Self:* The body.
3. *Emotional Self:* Feelings, responses, reactions, impulses, mo-

tivations, urges, desires, appetites, conditioning, attitudes, subconscious mind, memory.

4. *Mental Self:* Thought, reasoning, relationships, logic, choice, ideas, knowledge, wisdom, perception, understanding, attention, concentration, will, conscious mind.

5. *Personal Self:* Soul, quality, essence, personality, personal identification, what we have made of ourselves, characteristics.

6. *Spiritual Self:* God in man, the Christ, Higher Self, individuality.

7. *Universal Self:* God, Infinite Intelligence, the One Source, Divine Mind, unity, wholeness, light, energy, Cosmic consciousness, silence.

This classification indicates our entire range of human expression from the lower, outer nature to the higher, inner nature. The relationship of the seven levels of the Self may be shown as follows:

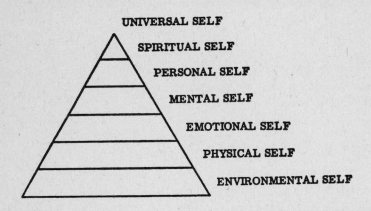

These classifications are not separate in themselves. They merely indicate different aspects of the complete person which you are. These various levels of yourself interpenetrate each other like this.

Actually, there is no place where one level of our nature leaves off and the other begins. We are one—but made up of parts. When these parts are properly related, we become an integrated being. We achieve this integration by understanding ourselves and by indentifying each level with the Universal Self at the center of our being. As we identify ourselves with the inner wholeness, we achieve balance, harmony and integration on every level of our expression. The process is one of *alignment,* which means travelling upward and inward in consciousness from the environmental level through to the universal and back down again. Visualize a current of energy flowing through every level of your being from the One Source. Visualize the circles below, and direct your mind as follows:

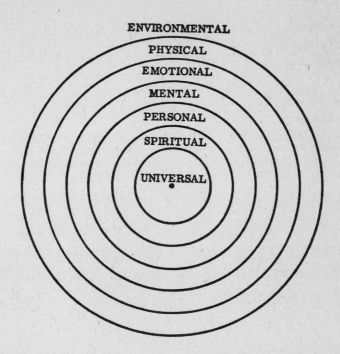

Environment

I now direct my consciousness upward and inward as I withdraw my attention from the world around me. I withdraw my attention from all circumstances, situations, problems and conditions as I let my mind go free and refill itself from the Divine Light within.

Body

As I travel upward and inward through the physical level, I recognize my body as an instrument of the Spirit. Every organ and function is in perfect order. I experience perfect circulation, perfect assimilation and perfect elimination as I align my body with the vital healing forces of the Infinite Mind.

Emotions

I am transformed by the renewing of my mind. I am attuned to the inner vibrations of wholeness. I identify myself with my natural state of balance and harmony. Everything unlike the nature of God is removed from my attitudes and feelings as I align myself with peace and love. I am emotionally mature.

Intellect

My mind is alert and clear as I recognize its place in the alignment of my total being. I think logically and I reason clearly. I exercise my power of choice wisely. I know many things. I have complete understanding. I concentrate my attention upon specific objectives and purposes. My will power is aligned with the Supreme Will of life. I give thanks for my marvelous mind.

Soul

"Build thee more stately mansions, O my soul!" I am the essence of all good things as I align my soul with the higher forces within me. My soul is awakened and attuned to the influx of spiritual nourishment. This great person within my body is free to develop and grow. I have a pleasant personality. I am identified with love. My soul embodies all desirable qualities. I make the most of myself, as my soul is the repository of all that is fine and good.

Higher Self

As I travel upward and inward in consciousness I am aligned with the Christ within me. I bring my gift to the altar in dedication and worship. I enter the temple of the Holy Spirit. I am one with my higher self. I dedicate myself to the service of the Most High. I am a point of light within the mind of God. I dwell in the kingdom of heaven. I am identified with my own divinity. I am an individual expression of God. I am a resident of the kingdom of heaven. I dwell in the secret place of the Most High.

God

I now reach the level of total identification. I am unconditioned by thought, feeling, time or space. I experience total being. "I and God are One." I float free in the upper reaches of Spirit. I am one with all light and energy. I am attuned to the cosmic forces of the universe. I encompass the cosmos. I experience illumination. I understand the secret of creation. I am cleansed. I am reborn. I am a native of eternity. I am.

As we reach the apex of the triangle, or the center of the circle of being, whichever way we are visualizing our journey into total consciousness, we become completely identified with the Whole. This has a profound effect upon us. Spiritual insights and deeper meanings accompany this adventure in divine inspiration. Powerful forces flow into us as our minds are released from petty concerns.

As we reach the highest point of inspiration, we will want to be completely still and immerse ourselves in the perfect bliss of the peace and unity which we feel. At this point we feel like a drop of water in a great and peaceful ocean, as a cell within the great body of God, or as a bright and shining star within the great galaxies of the heavens.

This entire experience will have a vitalizing and ennobling effect upon every part of your being. You will be inwardly transformed, and your mind, your body, and your worldly experiences will reflect the change. Each time you take this upward journey you will experience new and ever-expanding consciousness. You are exchanging personal limitations for the freedom of eternity and infinity. This alignment is the most valuable of spiritual techniques. It embodies all the others.

Whatever spiritual growth I myself have achieved is directly attributable to this exercise and what has evolved from it. The twelve points in the master plan of this book are an outgrowth of constant practice of this discipline over a period of years. You will achieve great results by its use.

How the "Raying-Out" Process Can Benefit You

Now for the second part of the technique of alignment. This is called the "raying-out process." As you reach the high point of Universal Consciousness you will become very quiet and, finally, completely silent. You will experience the "peace that passeth all understanding."

In this euphoric state you will experience complete well-being. Your conscious mind will be completely stilled and a heightened awareness will envelop you. Vital and dynamic feelings will pulsate through you as you are recharged by the cosmic forces. Light and energy will flow freely through every part of you. You will see the Light and become one with it. You will feel that at last you know God. You will achieve a release and a perspective which will free you from the bondage of human limitations forever.

You will probably not achieve the results I have described the first time, but as you repeat the process, you will begin to receive the desired response. Let yourself go and travel this golden ladder into freedom and power.

After a period of complete silence, which will vary in length, gradually begin to direct the flow of energy and light back down through the various levels of awareness until you again reach the outer level of environment and worldly experience. You may just silently visualize this as taking place, or you may speak out loud. My recommendation is to do it aloud, at least at first.

The "raying-out technique" goes something like this, as you again traverse the seven levels, this time in reverse order:

Universal

> Quietly now, I reside in the realm of pure light. Strength and power indwell me as I identify myself with the One Source from which all things flow. I am filled with divine energy. I feel the flow of Infinite Power through my entire being. I am the channel through which divine inspiration flows. I consciously direct the forces of the Infinite Potential into every level and every area of my life. I am a co-creator with God. I individualize omnipotence. I am omniscient, omnipresent and omniactive. I am at home with the One. I speak as my total Self.

The Christ

> The light and energy of Infinite Mind are raying out into the Higher Self. The Universal is individualizing itself through me. My Spiritual Self is awakened by the Light which is flowing into it. I am infused with light. I am alive. I am created whole and perfect. I am made in God's image. I have conscious divine intelligence. The Christ within me knows all things. The pure white light of Spirit is resident within my heart. I am perfect even as my God in Heaven is perfect. I have innate divinity. I am a point of light within the mind of God. I dedicate myself to the service and the expression of the One. I am aligned with the forces of good, truth and beauty. I am an outlet from the infinite reservoir of Spirit. I know my true identity now.

The Soul

Light and energy flow into my soul. I am awakened. "I lift up mine eyes unto the hills from whence cometh my help." I am ready to go about God's business. My soul is inspired from above and warmed by interest and cooperation from below. I am permanently identified with the Higher Self. I am in focus with the true picture of my self. Everything which happens contributes to the growth of my soul. I am constantly evolving and growing. Presence and principle meet in my soul. Spirit and Law are one as I evolve into a complete being. I learn my lessons well. I am instructed from above and the lessons of life are ingrained in my soul. I am an evolved being. I am a disciple of the Holy Quest. I seek. I find. I learn. I live. I love. I am at peace. I express gentle graciousness. I am kind. I am pure. I learn my lessons through discipline and experience. I function mentally, emotionally and physically. Through all experience I am guided by Divine Spirit. "In my Father's house are many mansions." I am at home in my Father's house today and always.

The Mind

Light is raying down into my mind. I am awakened to my magnificent potential. The cells of my brain are lighted with inspiration and enlightenment. I shine with heavenly radiance. I am a scintillating being. I am awakened. I am aware. I praise my mind as a magnificent instrument. I choose wisely and well. I reason perfectly. I think truly. My mind is the clearing house for great ideas. Concepts of inherent greatness guide my thoughts. I am an instrument in the great symphony of life. My mind connects heaven and earth. Through my mind, Divine Intelligence is translated into form and experience. I have access to all knowledge. I understand all things. I sustain my spiritual identity at all times. I am wise and understanding. My mind is both disciplined and flexible. My mind is my use of God's mind. My will is God's will—the Will of Life—the will of joyous experience. My mind chooses the true way of life and I live it fully now.

Feelings

As the Light rays down through the Higher Self, into my soul, through my mind, I feel it and respond to it. My sub-conscious mind is cleansed and ordered. All congestion is cleared and I am an open channel for the free, full flow of life. I am attuned to all that is true, lovely, and of good re-port. I am pure love. I respond strongly to all that is good. I react creatively to the higher awareness which flows through me. All confusion is healed. I put myself involun-tarily under the dominion of Truth. I have deep and abiding faith. I cooperate completely with the Law. I keep my "heart with all diligence; for out of it are the issues of life." There are no cross purposes. I flow with the strong currents of vital life. I have appetite only for that which is sweet and pure. I surge with love. I desire only that which is for the best interests of everyone concerned. I channel the Creative Power into constructive purposes. I know who I am and where I am going. I love life and I live it joyously now.

Body

The vital energies flow into my body, cleansing, healing and nourishing it. My blood stream carries the current of life to every cell. My body scintillates with energy. I am a radiant being. I express perfect health. I am a whole being. My body vitally expresses my wholeness. I am attuned to dynamic action. Divine life pulsates through my veins. My heart beats in rhythm with the heart of God. Universal cre-ative forces are manifested in my body. My body is a liv-ing temple. My body is Spirit in form. I respect my body. I take good care of it. I use it sensibly. I treat it well. Every organ reflects an aspect of the Perfect Whole. Through my spiritual dedication, and through right thought and reaction, every organ and function of my body is maintained in perfect focus with the Divine Pattern. Every function of my body represents God in action. I am healthy. I am whole. God is blessing my strong and beautiful body now. I give thanks for this magnificent instrument with which I move to accomplish God's purposes.

Expression

The Light rays out now into my world of affairs. Everything I do represents God in action. Everything I have is Spirit in form. My every experience is evidence of the working of the creative Law. I affirm order, harmony and right action. I look out upon my world and I find it good. My world represents my concept of God. I am surrounded by beauty. I am aligned with purposeful action. I am dedicated to good works. I give thanks for every experience. I bless every problem and difficulty, because it is through them that I learn and grow. I move freely through all conditions and circumstances. That which is within me is greater than that which is in the world. I become free from situations when I become free in them.

I give thanks for the many things which grace my world. I use them wisely. I am a good steward. I share whatever I have. I give freely of myself. I am God's instrument for doing good. I am love in action. I love my fellow man, individually and collectively. I do everything I can to help every one I meet. I love and I am loved. I experience perfect relationships at all times.

I am a successful person. It is my function to do the very best job of living that I can manage. By cooperating with the Spiritual Law, I bring my entire world of experience into focus with the perfect whole picture of order and right action. I am grateful for the privilege of being alive. And so it is.

Constant practice of this alignment technique will change your life as you become identified with your true self on every level. Go through these steps now, using your own words; make this valuable tool your own. Identify yourself and live according to your own specifications. You will be assisted by tremendous inner forces when you identify yourself with them.

Go back over this chapter now, reviewing the techniques and explanations which will help you identify yourself with what you want to be and what you want to do. They work. I know.

DAILY GUIDE TO IDENTIFICATION

Today I am identified with all that is noble, good and true. My identity is clear to all. I am a spiritual being, made in the image and likeness of God. I am eternally identified with the whole and the perfect. I am a native of eternity. In eternal life I live and move and have my being. There is no place where the Infinite leaves off and I, the individual, begins. We are one with each other. I am an expression of the Infinite Mind. I am identified with that which is greater than I.

I recognize good everywhere. I identify myself with all the good and constructive things of life. My mind dwells upon the noble ideas and I am ennobled by them. I identify myself with happiness. I am good, therefore I am happy. I identify myself with those thoughts and actions which bring happiness. I identify myself with good deeds. I participate in worthy projects which bring good to others. I and my brother and sister are one. I am identified with them. We are identified with the human race. We need each other. We help each other. We are identified with love and sharing. We live to serve God and our humanity.

I am identified with love. My heart is warm, my intentions are clear, and my motives are pure. I love life. I love people. I love work. I love to learn and grow. I am identified with that which I love. I expand my circle of love today. I love success. I identify myself with success on every level. God loves a successful person. I am a success as a person. I am successful in my work. I am successful in my relationships with other people. I am a well-balanced individual.

I am identified with health on every level of my being. I have a sound mind in a sound body. Spirit, mind and body are properly related to make me a whole person. I am identified with peace and freedom. I am identified with the finest, best, highest and noblest of human expression.

I am one with God. I am one with Life. I am one with truth and beauty. I express them in everything I do. I am identified with noble goals and ambitions. Every project I undertake is constructive and worthwhile.

I am aware of my true identity today. And so it is.

9

❖ ❖ ❖

Nothing Is Too Good to Be True

I recall a certain breakfast I had many years ago at the Great Northern Hotel in New York with Isabel Heaps, a wonderful Bible and Science of Mind teacher from Evanston, Illinois. I had asked for her guidance and advice. I sought a lot of it in those days. I was trying to find myself in the midst of the new ideas which the Science of Mind had given me, but I had not yet put together the whole picture. I had not yet convinced myself that I could do what I wanted to do. I needed assurance, and Isabel helped me find it.

As you know, Dr. Raymond Barker had started the whole thing several months before when he had told me, "You ought to get into this work. You'd be great."

Although I had a strong desire to do so, I had a great problem. That problem was myself. I couldn't see how I could make the transition from actor to minister. I needed a substantial income to meet my obligations, but now I wanted to change professions and I couldn't see how I could do it. I had been acting in television while I was studying and lecturing, but I knew the time was approaching for a showdown.

The more I became interested in teaching the Science of Mind, the less interested I was in acting. Even then I knew that you can't succeed in something you are not interested in. But I forgot that this law of cause and effect works constructively also: *You are bound to succeed in that which you are interested in.*

You will recall the four steps of accomplishment:

1. Get clearly in mind what you want.
2. Develop a conviction that it is already yours.
3. Do everything you can to bring it about.
4. Release it, give thanks and let it happen.

Chapters 7 and 8 presented the techniques for helping us develop the basic attitudes of *intention* and *identification* as part of our over-all twelve steps on the Ladder of Accomplishment. In the present chapter and in Chapter 10 we will be dealing with the techniques for Point 2—"Develop a conviction." We are now ready for this step. And so was I, in my evolvement toward becoming a teacher and a minister. I needed conviction—that inner certainty of mind and heart which knows that you *can* do what you want to do.

Learn to Make Up Your Own Mind

The world and other people aren't going to be nearly as excited about your dreams and ambitions as you are. Even your family and friends will think of a thousand reasons why you can't do what you want to do, and unless you are careful you yourself will think of a thousand more. Don't seek advice about what you should or should not do. This is no one's business but your own. If you don't know yourself, how can anyone else know?

It is my conviction that we succeed in spite of the advice of friends rather than because of it. Seek knowledge, instruction and advice about how to do a specific thing, but never about whether or not you should do it. Go ahead with it. Even your mistakes and fail-ures may be valuable to you, perhaps more than initial success. You are entitled to the total experience. Claim it and go to it. Do what-ever you need to do to succeed; just be sure that you don't hurt any-one else in the process. True, you may hurt yourself, but you are entitled to learn and grow from that experience too.

We are always confronted with decisions. We must always make a choice. There is always a right road and a wrong one. We are given the opportunity to choose the right one, but when we take the wrong one, it is right for us because we need the experience of the detour. In this sense, there are no mistakes, only wrong turnings. But eventually all roads lead up the mountain of fulfillment. We all get there, no matter how lost we may become, no matter how tortuous the way.

Constantly strengthen your inner conviction with mental and spiritual disciplines such as those given in this book. Keep ever before you that which you want to achieve. Constant affirmation will lead to conviction and acceptance. Clear thinking and deep feeling work together to form a strong subjective pattern for your desired good upon which the Creative Law may work. Only you can do the thinking and feeling which are necessary ingredients for achievement. There are no short cuts.

The directions outlined in this book are specific and definite. I guarantee that if you follow them, your life will change for the better and you will get where you want to be. I am not giving advice. I am showing you a way of life which brings results. It has worked for me. It will work for you if you learn it and use it. Keep at it.

"God won't show you the right way, but He will never let you take the wrong one." This advice was once given me by a wise teacher a number of years ago.

"What shall I do?" I had asked. "Please tell me what I should do. I don't know which way to turn."

But he was adamant. He would give me no advice. He forced me to go within myself for the answer to my questions as to what I should do and where I should go. He talked to my wife and me for hours, teaching us to develop our own inner resources through prayer, but when I tried to get him to make decisions for us he would only say, *"God won't show you the right way, but he will never let you take the wrong one."*

I wasn't sure what he meant, but this statement of spiritual truth gave me the courage to make my own decisions. Many of them were wrong ones, but something invariably corrected them and got me back on the right track. And I was all the better for having learned from the experience.

The following episode will show you what I mean.

Bernice and I were on a trip to California, trying to decide whether we wanted to go there to accept a ministry or to stay in the East. That's why we were seeking advice.

Finally we made up our minds. We decided to accept the ministry of the Religious Science Church in Santa Barbara, effective as soon as we could wind up our affairs in New York. I could hardly wait to get started on the big adventure—my first real church on my own. I had steadily been building my conviction of myself as a minister and I was ready to get started. But it seems we are always given a choice to see if we really mean what we think and say we do.

In the midst of moving preparations I was offered the lead in a Broadway play. I went ahead and signed for it, then told Bernice about it.

"But we had decided to go to Santa Barbara!" she exclaimed. "You gave your word. You can't change your mind now!"

"I haven't changed my mind," I affirmed. "We'll just postpone it a little while. This is a great opportunity, dear. It's a great part, and I'd like to wind up my career with a hit. Don't you understand what this means to me?"

"Well, I'll go along with what you want to do," my wife said. "But I think it's a mistake. I just hope the church in Santa Barbara will wait for you."

"So do I," I replied. "I'll write and ask them to wait for us a few months. I'll leave the play at the end of the season and we'll be in Santa Barbara in early summer."

On the day of the first rehearsal, as I was leaving our apartment for the theatre, a letter arrived from Santa Barbara. Rev. Thomas Baird, the retiring minister, had been taken suddenly ill and I was needed at once!

"Why, I can't do this play," I exclaimed to Bernice. "They need us in Santa Barbara."

"I'm afraid you'll have to, dear. You made the choice, didn't you?" she chided gently.

"Yes I did," I agreed reluctantly. "Look, call Santa Barbara and see how long they can wait. I have to run. I can't be late for the first rehearsal."

I arrived on time, and all the exciting machinery of a new Broadway production got under way; but somehow my heart wasn't in it.

This was the fulfillment of my lifetime ambition—the lead in a Broadway play—but the thrill wasn't there. My heart was elsewhere—in a tiny church in Santa Barbara.

The result was inevitable. As I was leaving the theatre after a dismal run-through rehearsal toward the end of the second week, with the road tryout opening only days away, the producer called me back and gave me the pink slip which ended my Broadway career forever. I accepted the dismissal without a word and somehow found my way uptown to our apartment, where Bernice found me staring silently into space when she came in several hours later.

"How was the rehearsal?" she asked, then stopped short as she saw my face. "What's the matter, dear?"

She put her arm around me anxiously. I just looked at her.

"Oh," she said quietly. "So now it's Santa Barbara. Is that it?"

I was on the plane that night and arrived in Santa Barbara in time for Sunday's service. And except for vacations, I haven't missed one since.

"God won't show you the right way, but He will never let you take the wrong one."

I had learned my lesson—the hard way. Once putting your hand to the plough, there is no turning back. Once you have made your decision and reached a conviction concerning it, you must follow through. Once you have sent your dream into orbit you must go along for the ride. When you reach the decision as to what you want and develop a strong conviction that it is already done, all the creative forces of the universe work to make it a fact. Once you have subconsciously accepted an idea, the Creative Law works on it to completion whether you are thinking about it consciously or not.

Our difficulties arise when we have subconsciously accepted two opposing ideas. We must make peace between them or there is nothing but trouble inside and outside.

My experience of wavering between the Broadway play and my call to the ministry was inevitable and necessary because of the two great objectives with which I had conditioned my mind. First was the desire to be an actor, plus my actual experience as one. This had been going on for over twenty-five years before I had even thought of being a minister. I had certainly established conviction, if not complete attainment as far as being an actor was concerned. As long as I had this strong identification and conviction, all the forces of nature were working to bring about complete success. The only thing that could block this success was my own negativity—doubt about my ability, worry about financial security, fear of failure, belief in irregularity of employment, and a hundred other things. We can be successful only to the degree that we dissolve the inner negatives.

But at this point I had brought a new element into my consciousness—a strong desire to do something else and a strong conviction that I *could* do it. My desire to be a minister had been growing, and my identification and conviction were reaching the point where some action was inevitable.

As I told you, I had made the decision to go to the church in Santa Barbara, then reversed it by accepting the lead in the play. Something has to give when two strong opposing forces are in conflict. It did. I was fired, and something picked me up and set me down in Santa Barbara. This, however, was where I belonged at that time. And the cause for all this was within my own mind. When I got my attitudes and beliefs straightened out, the outer picture of my experience cleared.

In fact, as time went on, I found that the actor and the minister were *not* in conflict, for I continued to be both for several years. I regularly commuted from my church in Santa Barbara to motion picture and TV work in Hollywood. The actor made the minister possible in many ways. The actor had, in fact, not been eliminated at all, just transformed. I am truly grateful for my twenty years as an actor every time I deliver a lecture, or speak on radio or television.

Remember, we would not *have* a particular goal if we were not capable of *accomplishing* it. Develop your conviction that this is true, *because it is.* Man was made for victory, not defeat. Use your human will to focus upon your objective, sustain your attention, but then take all human will power and effort out of the picture. The creative power within you will accomplish the rest.

Remember:

1. Something wonderful is happening to somebody all the time.
2. All of these wonderful things are coming from Infinite Mind.

3. This great Mind is within each one of us waiting to respond to our thought.

4. The great Law of Mind will produce for you your every desire once you accept it through identification and conviction.

During my years of study for the ministry in New York I became interested in clergymen and churches the same way I had once been primarily interested in actors and plays. This was quite a switch for me, for I hadn't been inside a church in years. In addition to attending classes and giving my own metaphysical talks, I went to hear every speaker I had time for, sometimes several in one day. It didn't matter what the denomination or creed was. I attended temples, cathedrals and synagogues. I became friends with teachers, ministers, priests and rabbis. I heard them all, and at the same time attended lectures and conferences on psychology, psychiatry and philosophy. I read everything I could get my hands on pertaining to scientific religion; I prayed and meditated for regular periods each day and often far into the night. All of this was scheduled around the busiest years I ever knew as an actor, for I appeared in several hundred television plays during TV's exciting early years.

At the same time, I was building a lot of identification and conviction during this period. Although I watched and listened carefully to my teachers and the many speakers whom I heard, I never tried to copy them. I was identifying myself with what they were doing, just as I had in the theatre in earlier years when I attended so many plays. As the identification grew, my conviction strengthened that I *could* do the thing I now wanted to do more than anything else—to become a teacher of the Science of Mind, to have my own church, and teach my own classes.

Soon tremendous results unfolded in my life. I was in a constant state of elation over the tremendous potential which was revealing itself to me. But I was unable to see how I could transfer from one profession to the other. This created a conflict in my mind. Even though I looked to show business to provide the income I felt I needed, I began to resent the time I had to give to it. Television, with its crime shows and commercials, just didn't do anything for me any more. I decided to make the change, but I still didn't know how. This is when I sought help from Isabel Heaps, whom I mentioned at the beginning of this chapter.

She listened with interest as I told her of my ambition, and she helped me decide on a simple plan. It is stated in this affirmation which we worked out together:

> This is a specific spiritual treatment for Donald Curtis of New York City. I know who I am and what I am doing. I am unfolding spiritually and I am growing in understanding and wisdom. My every thought and action move me one step closer to being that which I want to be—a teacher and minister of the Science of Mind. My studies at the Church of Religious Science and my own lectures give me the knowledge and experience I need. My individual counseling work develops love and compassion within me. I forget myself in my dedication to others. I am a minister in every sense of the word. Everything works together to move me surely and permanently toward achieving this goal. The financial means are available to make it possible for me to complete my studies and experience and to become firmly established as a teacher and minister. Every obligation is met on every level. There is the one right acting job for me which provides sufficient income to meet all of my requirements. This job is permanent and allows ample time for me to carry on my studies and lecturing. This job wants me as much as I want it. This job needs me as much as I need it. I give to this job what it needs and it provides me with what I need. It is mine. I accept it. I give thanks for it. I know that it is done. And so it is.

I constantly affirmed the ideas of this treatment during the next two or three months. Then I met Bill Warwick, a New York advertising executive, on the street one day. He invited me to come up to his office to see about a part on a new radio program.

To make a long story short, I became "the doctor" on a daytime radio serial, *The Doctor's Wife*. Manya Starr, a top radio and television writer, had remembered me from a TV audition months before, and had asked for me for the part.

The program was an instantaneous success and was a completely wonderful experience for the nearly two years it was on the air. From this one engagement I received more income than I had averaged in my free-lance television work, which had taken almost all of my time. Since we only rehearsed for an hour before each show, I was able to devóte all of my remaining time to my studies, lectures, and counseling work.

The treatment affirmation which Isabel and I had worked out had been demonstrated completely. There wasn't the slightest doubt in my mind, and there isn't now, that the working out of all events according to plan came about directly because of the scientific treatment work which was done on the situation. It always does when we build the inner mental equivalent of the whole picture of what we want to achieve, identify ourselves with it, and sustain a strong inner conviction that it is already true. The Creative Law *must* produce what we completely accept mentally and emotionally. This is the scientific basis of the entire Science of Mind teaching.

You have seen how it worked for me. It is working in the lives of hundreds of thousands of people who are using these principles and techniques today. It can work for you. Nothing is too good to be true; nothing is too wonderful to happen.

In reading about how things have worked out for me as the result of scientific prayer treatment work, I know that many of you may say, "Oh, it would have worked out that way anyway." Perhaps, but perhaps not. It is all right just to let things happen if you don't care what happens. But if you want to give purpose, meaning and direction to your life, you have a definite part to play in the creative process. We are now working upon *conviction,* that inner certainty of mind which gives power and direction in the creative forces. When thought and feeling blend together in an attitude of conviction, you will have confidence in yourself and faith in something greater than you are.

As you review the previous chapters of this book, you will see that each step blends together with the succeeding ones and culminates in forming the attitude which we are discussing at the moment. *Con-*

viction is the culmination of the previous seven steps. They are all parts of the whole picture. The remaining four steps following conviction will each be the result of the total of the previous ones. Complete fulfillment comes only when there is a constant interplay of all of these twelve basic attitudes. Let's understand each one in turn, and then we will put them all together at the conclusion of the book.

It is my conviction that the basic ingredients of the system described in this book are at work within the minds of every one of us whether we are consciously aware of them or not. They must be. It is not my intention to inject anything into our spiritual makeup that is not already there. The purpose is to make us aware of our magnificent potential and to understand how it works.

True, there are many people who live very effectively without consciously knowing anything about these things, but you can rest assured that there is a subconscious attunement with the process; otherwise there would be no results. The twelve steps of our process add up to the effective functioning of the whole person. If you have achieved this, you do not need this book except as, I hope, an interesting account of the way our creative faculties work. For the rest of us who may not be quite so far along in our evolvement, it will give us a system whereby we may develop our magnificent potential and experience richer, fuller lives.

I can see, in presenting this spiritual autobiography, how immature my own early efforts to comprehend and apply these principles really were. I can see, for instance, that my motives were often much too self-centered. I can see how I lacked real faith, and endeavored to make things happen rather than cooperating with principle. I can see how I was often much more interested in getting what I wanted rather than in giving what was needed. But all of these things work out eventually. We can only operate on our own level of understanding. The point is to keep growing in understanding and to see that we constantly make better the best that we can do.

It was only after I had been a minister for some years that I began to get the slightest glimmer of what it means to be one. It is obvious as I read back over my intention, identification and conviction steps in becoming a minister that I was motivated by a personal desire, by what it might mean to me as a means of self-expression and attainment, rather than by higher motives. Perhaps as an actor I merely fancied myself in a new role which appealed to me. I don't really know. I do know that the conviction was strong and I was moved steadily along into its attainment.

Let me also point out that we must all start where we are. Life is a refining process. If we were all frightened by the mistakes we might make or the difficulties of attaining our ambitions, no one would ever get anywhere. Get clearly in mind what you want to do, develop your conviction concerning it, then do it with as much understanding and effectiveness as possible.

If you make a mistake or fail, find out what you did wrong, learn the lesson, correct your procedure, and keep going. Life is always on the side of the person who lives according to principle.

And yet, principle often gets lost in practice. The experiences of the world often blur our vision and separate us from our objectives and our convictions. It almost happened to me.

My radio show, *The Doctor's Wife,* was an immediate success and grew in popularity as the months rolled by. Contracts were renewed and salaries raised, and we all assumed that the program would go on forever. I myself began to take it for granted, playing my role "off the top of my head," while I dedicated my real efforts toward lecturing, teaching and counseling. I had completed my required studies by this time, had my credentials as a practitioner, and soon had a full schedule of daily appointments with those who came to me for help.

At this time, Bernice and I had just been married. We lived comfortably in a lovely uptown apartment, our classes and lectures in Philadelphia were growing, and life was very good indeed. This went on for some months, and the pattern of our existence became fairly well set. In a sense, "I had it made." But I was getting a little too comfortable too soon.

One scorching summer afternoon I came into the comfortably air-conditioned studio for rehearsals. Then I stopped short. The cast was seated glumly around the table with their scripts before them; there was hardly an acknowledgment as I greeted them.

"What's the matter?" I asked. "Has the show been canceled?"

Ordinarily this would have brought a laugh. Sponsors don't drop shows as popular as *The Doctor's Wife*. We all assumed that we could go on forever. But today something was wrong. I soon found out what it was.

"You guessed it," the director nodded. "We go off Monday."

"You're kidding," I ventured. "Why? What happened?"

"Change of policy. Sponsor's going in for TV," was the reply.

"Why, darling, what's the matter?" Bernice asked as I walked dejectedly into our apartment half an hour later. "Has the show been canceled?"

"Goes off Monday," I grunted as I sank into a chair. "What do you think of that?"

"Well—," Bernice said as she put her arm around me. "I suppose it had to happen sometime. I'm sure it's all for the best. Let's do some treatment work on it, shall we?"

We prayed—for a long time.

Finally, there came a deep sense of inner peace. The hard, cold knot of fear dissolved from my stomach, and as my head cleared, I could see the whole picture clearly.

Of course *The Doctor's Wife* experience had to end. I wasn't an actor any more; I was a minister. I had become one through the intensity of my own inner conviction—no matter how much the actor's ego, the smaller self, had resisted it. I had let myself become soft and complacent with the comfort of surface success. I had forgotten the specifications of the affirmation out of which this experience came into my life—so that I could dedicate myself to higher purpose. Now the time had come. The idea was ready to happen.

All of these things and many more came to me during those hours of prayer that night. *Prayers are always answered.* We just need to listen. As Bernice and I spoke and listened, we came to see the whole picture there in the gathering dusk. Our lives took on a new dimension and our hearts were filled with new purpose and conviction. Even though I had worked toward the ministry perhaps without receiving a definite "call," I believe I came close to getting it that night. I know I have received it since, and it increases in clarity and intensity as the years go by.

UNDERSTANDING TREATMENT—AND WHAT IT CAN DO FOR YOU

In this book we have frequently mentioned "treatment," "scientific prayer," "prayer treatment," "affirmative prayer," and other similar terms.

In the larger sense, your every thought and feeling is your prayer. In the specific sense, prayer is conscious contact with the Supreme Power. *Treatment* is that consciously-directed spiritual and mental process which achieves a specific result.

In this sense, we use the words "treatment" and "prayer" interchangeably as long as the prayer is an affirmative one. Prayer, of course, should always be affirmative. Effective treatment must always be based upon the spiritual premise that there is a Presence and a Power within us that becomes the thing we desire, to the extent that we accept this as being true. Thus, treatment is the process of getting our objectives clearly in mind and removing all doubts and reservations concerning their achievement. The goal of treatment is a sustained affirmative attitude of mind—*conviction.*

Treatment dissolves fear and affirms faith. Treatment is an inner process of the mind, consciously directed until it is accepted at the subconscious level. Once it is completely accepted subconsciously it works automatically as part of the Creative Law. We all have this subconscious conviction about some things, but need to develop it about others. Wherever we encounter doubt or fear in our thoughts and feelings, we dissolve these negatives and affirm the more constructive attitudes of conviction and faith.

In its simplest form, treatment is the process of making affirmative statements until we accept them. There are many techniques of treatment. This book presents an over-all approach to the process, plus many specific techniques for developing it. Treatment means convincing yourself of the reality of a desired good. Treatment is the process of reaching conviction.

The test of whether or not you have reached true conviction is whether or not *you really believe what you want to believe.* Conviction is *knowing,* ingrained so deeply that your mind accepts the idea completely and cannot conceive of its opposite.

Not only is the attitude of conviction essential for the effective working of the creative process within you; it also has a magnetic effect upon other people and attracts their help and cooperation. The strength of my wife's conviction that we could build our home finally moved me from negative to positive, from lukewarm to hot, from doubt to conviction.

There is no way to resist being moved by the consciousness of a person who believes his idea is the greatest idea in the world. There is a sweep and a grandeur about a person who really believes what she is doing—who is absolutely convinced of the success of its outcome. When you are convinced, your enthusiasm and sincerity convince others; it's as simple as that.

Bernice and I were able to build our home in Santa Barbara because we caught on fire with the idea, and in so doing enlisted the aid of many people—bankers, builders, tradespeople and friends who helped us.

I have absolute conviction that the spiritual philosophy which I teach is the greatest thing in the world. I have long been convinced that it is the *hope* of the world. I know that when people learn to think straight, their lives and the entire world will straighten out. There is absolutely no limit to the good this teaching can do. It is a way of life which extends to all people. It transforms them by renewing their minds.

The fact that I owe my life to these principles, and the fact that I constantly see their practical effects in healing, adjusting, and changing people's lives for the better—these things fill me with sincerity and enthusiasm. I feel deeply about this teaching. I want to help people help themselves. You are the only person who can grow for you; you are the only person who can solve your problems; but I can help you by showing you the way. I intend to do so, and I am convinced that I can. I think I have fairly described the conviction and enthusiasm which motivates the several hundred of us who are teachers and ministers in the Religious Science Churches and in other New Thought groups. Our conviction, and the sound spiritual basis of our teaching, is an unbeatable combination.

This, I believe, is why people fill our churches and meeting halls, pack our classes, listen to our broadcasts, and read our magazines and books. We are giving people a solid set of practical spiritual principles to live by. We are convinced that this is so and people respond accordingly.

And so will people respond to you in whatever way you want them to when you strengthen your conviction.

Bernice was at one time one of the top insurance writers in New York City, doing a good deal of her selling on the telephone. She had an inner conviction that carrying adequate insurance was beneficial to people. She expected people to want what she had to offer. They did. The same affirmative inner attitudes made her a success later on when she sold real estate. My wife always had this inner conviction of success. She was always successful in everything she undertook. Outer success is an automatic result of affirmative inner attitudes. You can have similar success when you develop the affirmative attitudes presented in this book.

Years ago, one of the top general agents for life insurance was a self-made man who was once a sewer worker in New York. He remained one until he was nearly forty. As he was coming up out of a manhole one day he was driven back to cover by the splash from the wheels of a carriage as one of the silk-hatted gentry of the day went speeding past. Something clicked inside him as he wiped the mud from his eyes and climbed out, looking after the perpetrator of his indignity.

"What the devil has that guy got that I haven't got?" he asked himself. He pondered the incident as he went home and told his wife about it.

"Tell me," he demanded. "What *has* that fellow got that I haven't?"

"An education," his wife answered.

During the next three years he went to night school while continuing to work in the sewers. At the end of this time he opened his own insurance agency. When he retired twenty years later, his agency was writing over 100 million dollars' worth of life insurance a year. This man had reached a conviction about his own ability and capacity for success, and followed through with it.

Moreover, it was always his conviction that successful people like to do business with successful people. He saw to it that his salesmen maintained a conviction of success. If he found out that one of his men was having financial problems, or if he detected a hangdog look or an anxious manner, he called the man in and got to the heart of the matter. A master psychologist, this expert salesman inspired others with his conviction of success.

Affirmations and Denials—How to Get Rid of Negative Traits

Sit down right now and make a list of negative traits and attitudes that you would like to get rid of. The way to dissolve them is to develop a conviction of their opposite. When we "accentuate the positive" we "eliminate the negative." You will soon find that as you rid yourself of negative tendencies, the natural order of things will bring good into your life.

Use this technique of "denial and affirmation" whenever you detect a negative tendency. Keep a sharp lookout on what you think, feel, say and do. Put a plus or a minus sign in front of everything that comes up. If you says, "Gee, I feel terrible!" that is a minus. If you say, "Boy, I feel terrific!" that is a plus. If you think, "Life is a ball!" that is a plus. If you feel depressed, that is a minus. If you feel joyous and confident, that is a plus.

Do you see how it works? Make a game of it with yourself and play it with others who are trying to improve themselves. When the plus signs overbalance the minuses, you will be on your way to real accomplishment. You will be identified with and will be developing a conviction of right action as the plus factor increases.

Some of our inner negative attitudes are especially deep-rooted and require more intensive handling. This is done as follows, with you supplying your own particular list of inner problems to work upon. Note that we are working with mental and emotional beliefs and attitudes, not with outer conditions. These take care of themselves when we get right inside.

The following statement are examples only. If you wish, you may supply your own words. When making the statement of denial, do not dwell on the negative any more than is necessary. Simply pinpoint the negative for the purpose of denying it, then follow the denial with good strong statements of affirmation, as follows:

Fear——Faith

All fear is removed from my mind as I am now established in strong and enduring faith. All negative causation is dissolved from my consciousness as I think and feel constructively about all things. What do I have to be afraid of? Absolutely nothing. God is on my side. He has had His arm around me for a long time and He is never going to take it away. I have faith in a superior power which is always working through me. I trust in this power. I am strong in spirit, mind and body. I have complete faith today. And so it is.

Doubt——Certainty

There is no doubt in my mind but that I can be what I want to be, do what I want to do, and have what I want to have! All doubt of any kind is removed from my mind. I go purposely ahead with the certainty that all good things are working out in my life. I am cheerful and confident at all times. My attitudes are constructive. I believe in right action. I know that I am on the right track. I move forward with certainty and steadiness. I am sure of myself now. And so it is.

Suspicion——Trust

I expect the best from everything and everybody. I give myself and everyone else the benefit of the doubt. All suspicion is dissolved from my mind. I trust in God, I trust in myself, and I trust other people. I have the courage and strength of my convictions. I know that life offers me the best and I claim it as my own. I cooperate with others and I expect them to cooperate with me. I believe in the essential goodness of all people. I help them express their best today. I hurt no one and no one can hurt me. I am filled with trust now. And so it is.

Inferiority——Confidence

I am a capable person. All feelings of inferiority are removed as I develop confidence in myself. I am a good person. I am able to meet successfully all of life's challenges. I establish authority over myself and my actions. I will not be pushed around by doubts or fears. I dissolve them, and I establish authority in my world. I am confident at all times. I am capable of doing whatever it is that I am given to do. I am successful in all endeavors. I am a pillar of strength. I stand on a firm foundation. I am as solid as a rock. I am confident now. And so it is.

Hate——Love

There is no hostility in me. I dissolve all hatred by the action of love. All resentment disappears as I learn to understand and forgive. All criticism is removed as I learn to appreciate and approve. I love people. There is no condemnation in me. I look for the best, I expect the best, and I accept only the best at all times. I love everything and everybody. I love life and I love to live. I have no time for petty grievances. I am too busy expressing the love I feel in my heart. I am free today as I cover my world with love. I am a loving person now. And so it is.

Guilt——Forgiveness

I forgive myself. I dissolve all guilt and self-condemnation. I make amends for past mistakes, and I determine to commit no more in the future. I make peace with myself. I learn to love myself, and I determine to be the kind of person whom people can love. I have nothing against myself. I refuse to carry the burden of guilt. I free myself as I forgive myself. I am forgiven as I forgive. I start with myself. I act from pure motives and do my best to be my best at all times. I am at peace with myself, my world, and everyone in it. I am a whole person now. And so it is.

Irritation——Pleasantness

I am free from all pesky traits of character. I must and do cleanse myself of all irritation. There is no place for it in my life. I determine to be pleasant at all times. I am an easy person to get along with because I try to see everything from the other person's point of view. I am never annoyed. I look at all situations objectively and I endeavor truly to understand. When minor disturbances occur, I learn to say, "It doesn't matter just because it doesn't matter." I am calm, cool and collected at all times. I am a pleasant person now. And so it is.

Violence——Gentleness

All anger and antagonism are dissolved from my consciousness today as I adopt a kind and gentle attitude of mind. There is no place for violence in my life. I am a gentle person, with a sweet temper and disposition. I find out what is causing my eruptions and I eliminate them once and for all. Life is not taken by storm, but by the gentle and steady approach. I am calm and controlled at all times. I am relaxed inside and outside. I know how to let go and let life flow through me. I am gentle, kind and considerate. I live from the Higher Self today. And so it is.

Confusion——Peace

Today I know the meaning of peace of mind. I bring order out of confusion. I experience quiet instead of turbulence. I dissolve everything except serenity and tranquillity. I do not rush. I adjust myself to order and right timing. I do not run. I walk. I plan my actions in an orderly manner. I live ever in the temple of peace. "Only the finite has wrought and suffered; the Infinite lies stretched in smiling repose."* I am attuned to the Infinite now. I lie down in green pastures and I walk beside the still waters. I experience peace of mind and soul today. And so it is.

Conflict——Agreement

I remember that if I do not fight a thing I cannot lose. I stop fighting myself today as I bring all parts of my consciousness into agreement. I attain my true potential as I erase all inner conflict. I dissolve the blockages of negative states of mind, and I release all of my energy for constructive purposes. I cooperate with myself at all times. I channel all my energies toward the accomplishment of good. Argument becomes agreement. Doubt and fear become conviction and faith. I know no opposition to the free, full action of my true self. I am in agreement with life today. And so it is.

Cruelty——Kindness

I will never knowingly hurt another human being. Every tendency toward cruelty is dissolved from me once and for all. I am kind. I am loving. I do everything I can to help others. I cannot hurt others without hurting myself. I do everything I can to help everyone feel better. I have empathy for every living thing. I watch every word. I speak with love. I watch every deed. I act with love. Sympathy and love flow out from me and bless everyone I meet. I am kind and loving in my heart, and my world is filled with love and kindness. I am a kind and loving person now. And so it is.

Anxiety——Serenity

All tension and anxiety are removed from me as I relax, let go, and let happen. I know that all things proceed from the

* "Spiritual Laws," Ralph Waldo Emerson, Thomas Y. Crowell Company, New York, 1926.

quiet mind and I am immersed in quiet, calm, peace and silence. I am a disciple of the quiet way. I tap the well-springs of Infinite Power as I learn to be still and know that God is within me. I meditate upon the serenity of nature, and the order and beauty of the heavens as I become still inside and worship the wonder of life. My human will is one with Divine Will. I bask in quiet. I luxuriate in silence. I experience complete serenity now. And so it is.

This will give you some denials and affirmations to work on. The list is endless. Work upon those negative traits which apply to you. Be honest with yourself. Admit them, face them, and eliminate them. You don't need them, so let them go. You can actually rebuild your entire character systematically if you need to. Let nothing stand between you and the conviction that you really are the person you want to be. You will obtain your objectives in life when you remove the blockages within yourself that have held you back.

Now strengthen this conviction with:

DAILY GUIDE TO CONVICTION

There is one Power that flows through everything. There is one Intelligence that indwells all things. There is one Presence that embodies all things. This Something is the sum total of all good. It exists in me and I exist in It. Through this conviction I am strengthened. Through this conviction I grow. Through this conviction I become that which I am meant to be. Through this conviction I bring myself into focus with the larger pattern of my life. Through this conviction I become one with the total picture of good.

Today I am my complete, total and best self at all times. I am filled with confidence in myself and faith in the greater good. All fear is dissolved as my faith grows. All doubt is removed as my confidence grows. I am convinced that all wonderful things are true. Nothing is too good to be true. Nothing is too wonderful to happen. I am sure of my place in the great scheme of things. I have my right place in life and I fill this place with authority and conviction. I am a strong person. All weakness is dissolved as the inner strength flows through me. I am filled with power. I use this power wisely to accomplish good work. I never waver in my purpose. I know that all good is taking place through me right now.

My thoughts and feelings are married in vital conviction. My inner dynamic radiates through everything I think, say, feel and do. I am the master of every situation. I am motivated by noble purpose and ambition. I do noble deeds and dream noble dreams. The universe is mine and everything that is in it, and I am worthy of the trust. I use my inner power wisely and well. I am a credit to God, to the human race, and to myself. All limitation is removed from my consciousness once and for all.

I am strong. I am true. I am a whole person. The conviction of greatness emanates from my soul. It is my conviction that our destiny is oneness with God. I give thanks that this is so. And so it is.

10

❖ ❖ ❖

The Place Is Here;
The Time Is Now

The elderly lady across the desk stared at me hard and long for nearly a minute; then without a word she rose from her chair and walked unaided to the door.

As she opened it, she suddenly turned and gasped, "My crutches! Bring me my crutches! I'll fall. Quickly, quickly!"

She snatched the crutches from me as I brought them, adjusted them to her wrists and hobbled quickly down the hall without looking back. The elevator swallowed her up and she was gone. My first patient since I had become a practitioner of Religious Science had come and gone.

Slowly I turned back to my office and just stood there silently for a long time. I don't know who was more deeply affected, my patient or I. What had happened? She had walked by herself the half-dozen steps to the door after having told me that she had not moved without the aid of crutches for over twenty years. Now she had walked. What had really happened? Whatever it was it had frightened her, and to tell the truth, it frightened me, too.

So it was really true. Jesus had meant it when he said the lame should be made to walk and the blind to see. He proved this innumerable times, but He also said, "Sin no more, lest a worse thing come unto thee." We can be made whole through faith, but this faith must be sustained by an inner acceptance.

My patient and I had entered the kingdom, but we didn't believe that we belonged there. We weren't prepared to accept the gift which had been given, and so it was taken away. I was as much to blame as the crippled lady who had sought my help. I learned then, after giving my first treatment for another person, that the power we are working with is greater than anything we can conceive of. I also realized that we have very little to do with what happens after we have once released this power. We can recognize it, align ourselves with it, and direct its action, but what happens then is the result of the working of the inner Law, not of human effort.

This first patient of mine had been sick in mind and soul, as well as in body. She was filled with resentment, bitterness and self-pity. I explained to her that this could have a great deal to do with the crippling arthritis in her body. She rejected this, however, as she poured out her tale of woe and hatred toward certain members of her family whom she felt had treated her badly. I suggested that the tense situation might be alleviated if she could adopt a different attitude toward them and forgive them. I even went so far as to suggest that if we removed the hurt from her mind it would also disappear from her body. This she was not willing to do. But she had engaged an hour of my time, so I listened.

As I listened, I carried on my silent inner mental work, denying each negative as she brought it up, and affirming the opposite attitude, just as we did in the exercises at the close of the last chapter.

Gradually the woman's tirade subsided, as the effect of my treatment was felt. It was impossible to maintain an attitude of hostility if love and forgiveness are being affirmed. The practitioner's job is to see through the false picture presented by the person in trouble and to reach a realization of his wholeness and perfection. In scientific mental practice we discipline our minds to dissolve the outer problem by realizing the presence of good in its stead.

In this instance, I worked toward the realization that the crippling arthritis—the result of years of destructive attitudes of hatred, bitterness and resentment—was not real. It was a fact, but it was surely not the truth about the woman to whom it was attached.

I continued to work toward the realization of perfection with my patient. When she had talked herself out, I explained fully the principles which I have just been talking about here; then I suggested that we join together in prayer treatment, dissolving all of the hatred, resentment and bitterness, and affirming complete wholeness and perfection. I explained that when we reached that realization that this was true, we would get results, perhaps instantaneously. I explained that it was nothing I said or did, but that I was merely leading the way into realization, where Principle could take over.

We followed our verbal treatment of about ten minutes with a period of complete quiet during which our minds were held in focus upon the truths which had been spoken. We had reached a high state of consciousness in which complete realization was possible. There was absolutely no resistance. We were definitely aligned with the Higher Self.

It was enough to sustain the lady in complete normalcy as she walked to the door. It would have been enough to straighten and strengthen her crippled limbs for the rest of her life. But the old conditioning was too strong. The new realization was not sustained when she suddenly became aware that she was without her crutches.

When this troubled woman hobbled out of my office, that was the last I saw of her. And yet, for a few brief seconds, hadn't she walked without her crutches? I like to think that she remembers that moment of affirmation and success, and that in the years that followed she has put her own creative power to work more effectively.

This episode serves to point up one important question: can we be healed and enlightened by understanding and the practice of affirmative prayer or not? I know that we can. The way is to recondition the mind with affirmative attitudes, starting with the twelve basic ones developed in this book. This may entail a drastic change for some of us. However, I am convinced that *there is nothing that does not respond to or that cannot be completely healed through the power of prayer.* First, we must fulfill the conditions of effective prayer. There must be total assent of the mind. Total healing can only follow complete realization of inner perfection and wholeness, and this realization must be sustained.

In the case of my patient it was there—only for an instant to be sure—*but it was there.* I have since learned that this realization *can* be sustained, once it is reached, by continued conditioning of the mind in terms of it—in other words, the complete and continued development of our twelve basic mental attitudes. I have also learned that even though this realization may be slow in coming, we can work toward it and constantly improve in the process by living by these affirmative principles.

Do not be discouraged if you don't get immediate results. Keep at it. For some time, I myself have been working upon certain problems and conditions which have not yet responded. But here is the amazing thing about this process: Even though we do not achieve the specific results we strive for, our inner development of realization often brings about even more wonderful things—things we may never have dreamed of. I originally became interested in this affirmative spiritual process because I wanted help in solving my problems. Some got solved and some didn't, but working with these principles has changed my entire life, giving me an inner realization of beauty and wholeness, and moving me into my true life's work after I had spent years in floundering. This alone is enough to sell me on the idea. As you apply the principles which I am sharing with you in this book, you will move steadily and surely along the way to a realization of who and what you really are. Just apply yourself and keep applying yourself. Yes, it is a fact that you can heal yourself. Natural processes within the body are doing it all the time; otherwise we would all have been dead long ago. Healing is simply a matter of cooperating with the natural forces which are always at work to keep us whole and in balance. As you recondition your mind along the constructive pattern of our twelve steps, you will find many old conditions and weaknesses disappearing. As soon as we raise the inner consciousness, the outer conditions automatically respond.

Recently, for example, I started to develop the unmistakable symptoms of a cold. I had broken some physical laws and I knew it. Poor diet, insufficient rest and exercise, together with some tension and overwork, had physically weakened me. Yet I knew that the body is quick to respond to care and to prayer treatment. I quickly applied it and also took other necessary steps to correct the whole picture. I cleansed my body inside and out, engaged in some deep breathing exercises, and then gave myself a *specific* and *strong* prayer treatment for correction and for realization of perfect health. Then I piled into bed for a good long sleep. Next morning I awoke feeling as clear as a bell. Perfect cooperation of mind and body had done the trick. This is what I mean by approaching ourselves from the basis of the "whole person." My prayer treatment was for the purpose of renewing my realization of myself as a whole person— and it worked.

Now is the time for you to start making yourself a whole person. It doesn't matter what the problem is. Work toward the realization that God—wholeness and perfection—is already there. Specifically go through these five steps:

1. Develop your faith in a superior power.
2. Realize that what is true of it is true of you.
3. Have faith that it knows what it is doing.
4. Realize that the power is working specifically to correct your problem or fulfill your desire.
5. Rest in this realization. Stop worrying. Let go and let God work through you.

Under each of the five steps, develop your realization by the various means outlined in this book. Work specifically upon each one of the twelve basic attitudes. Calmly and quietly build your inner realization until your mind comes to a point of complete acceptance of the ideas you have been affirming.

Believe me when I say that a deep sense of peace will result from this process. When this inner peace arrives, be perfectly still and let the realization of inner power flow through you. Release all personal effort and let it happen. Remember, you are not doing it. You are co-operating, not coercing. That which works through you is greater than you are. Let *it* do the work.

Keep following through in this way until you get results. Use this approach while you are taking whatever outward steps may seem necessary at the time. Even if you are undergoing intensive medical therapy, assist the doctor with your own inner spiritual work. Everything works together in building the whole person. As your inner realization grows, the change will come about, and eventually you will find no further need for outer means.

It doesn't matter through what means the realization is reached, or what is said, or who says it. The important thing is to reach the realization. If you can reach it yourself, all the better. If you are too close to your problem to reach your own realization, it is important that you work with a practitioner or minister—someone who is not personally attached to the problem. The practitioner's job is to reach the realization of wholeness and perfection. Your job is to be receptive to it.

The Universal Subjective Mind, or Law, is present in all places simultaneously. It knows nothing about time, distance or place. It only knows how to respond in terms of what is known, no matter who knows it or where it is known. There is no such thing as "absent healing." The Law is ever-present. A practitioner can work as effectively for a patient halfway across the world as he can if he is in the same room with him. The only important thing is that a realization of truth be reached somewhere by someone.

I have before me my healing list of the many people for whom I am doing regular prayer treatment work. I work for them individually during regular morning and evening prayer periods, and at various times throughout the day as they come into my mind. These people often come to me with problems which they are unable to handle by themselves. My job is to maintain a constant realization of wholeness and right action about these people until the problem clears, the illness is healed, and the good is manifested. This method always gets results, sometimes almost miraculous and spectacular ones. In other cases the improvement is more likely to come about as a steady, progressive growth. It largely depends upon the realization of the practitioner being accepted and absorbed by the patient. The time of this varies, depending upon the amount of false belief that needs to be dissolved.

Now, I don't mean to imply that everyone is always healed or that all problems are eliminated. This would be a ridiculous claim. We are working with a scientific law of mental and spiritual causation. We really know very little about it except that it works. However, we do know that as we learn more about how to use it, the greater are the results. We also know positively that constructive attitudes of mind, released through strong faith and realization into spiritual Law, work as a healing force to overcome the ills and countless difficulties in which people find themselves.

The method we present here is a way to do something about our problems. No doubt we will always have some. Problems are the food of growth. But we can learn how to transcend them rather than surrender to them. We can consciously create circumstances. The knowledge of how to do this will make life vastly more pleasant and effective.

Moreover, individual causation lies within the individual mind. We need not be victims of environment or circumstances. We can rise above them. We can be transformed by the renewing of our minds. When we fully realize this we will do something about it. Actually, we have not yet begun to tap the magnificent potential which lies within us. It is time we started, don't you think? You and I are doing it right now through our absorption and use of these ideas. Let's determine to follow through in becoming that which we want to be, by overcoming all difficulties and rising to a realization of the True Self. This is the whole aim and purpose of life. It is truly a great adventure. Let's not deny ourselves the privilege of experiencing it fully.

The realization of this makes struggle, worry, hurry, pressure, tension and anxiety completely unnecessary. There is a great Being that loves us better than we love ourselves. There is that which knows what we have need of before we ask. There is a presence that heals. There is a power that eternally awaits our use of it. There is a life that lives forever. Illness, conflict, failure, limitation—even death—are all states of consciousness. When we resolve them back into life through a realization of truth, we live abundantly forever.

Our present life in the physical body is merely a phase of the larger life. We are here today and gone tomorrow, according to the normal human cycle, but we do not die. We are constantly expanding into new and larger levels of consciousness and expression. Our realization must ever be one of faith over fear, success over failure, happiness over misery, health over illness, abundance over lack, light over darkness, freedom over bondage—life over death.

This is what this book is about. This is the life's work for every one of us. This is the job of the practitioner, the minister and the teacher. As we all move together in this direction we will each be doing our part toward reaching the realization of full and abundant life.

HOW THE BIBLE CAN HELP YOU BUILD FAITH

The Bible is filled with guides to faith. Let's learn to understand and use them.

Consider such statements as these:

1. "Ask and it shall be given you; seek and ye shall find; knock, and it shall be opened unto you." (Luke 11:9)
2. "Your Father knoweth what things ye have need of before ye ask him." (Matt. 6:8)
3. "It is your Father's good pleasure to give you the kingdom." (Luke 12:32)
4. "If two of you shall agree on earth as touching any thing that ye shall ask, it shall be done for them of my Father which is in heaven." (Matt. 18:19)
5. "It shall be given you in that same hour what ye shall speak." (Matt. 10:19)
6. "What things soever ye desire, when ye pray, believe that ye receive them, and ye shall have them." (Mark 11:24)
7. "If ye abide in me and my words abide in you, ye shall ask what ye will and it shall be done unto you." (John 15:7)
8. "With God all things are possible." (Matt. 19:26)
9. "According to your faith be it unto you." (Matt. 9:29)
10. "So shall my word be that goeth forth out of my mouth: it shall not return unto me void, but it shall accomplish that which I please, and it shall prosper in the thing whereto I sent it." (Isaiah 55:11)

These are all strong statements of promise, faith and realization. There are hundreds of others in the Bible, all expressing how the Law of Mind works. The principles of the Bible are not the exclusive premise of organized religion. Your religion is your way of life. Free yourself of fear, guilt and superstition concerning it. Live it. Believe in something and build your life toward a realization of that which you believe. The above statements are scientific principles of applied psychology. They are meant to be used in the business of living. Try them.

The story of Jesus himself is a clear demonstration of how these principles work. He believed them implicitly, applied them, and explained them for all to use. There is no nonsense in the teachings of Jesus. They are all based upon scientific mental and spiritual principles which give us a realization and a pattern of action for effective living. The same principles that Jesus used to raise the dead, heal the sick, and multiply the loaves and fishes are available for us to use today. The twelve master points of this book are for the purpose of showing us how to do it.

REALIZATION THROUGH GIVING THANKS

"And he took the seven loaves and the fishes, and *gave thanks,* and brake them, and gave to his disciples, and the disciples to the multitude." (Matt. 15:36)

We are all familiar with the story of how Jesus fed the multitude of four thousand with seven loaves and a few small fishes. It is one that illustrates a basic principle: *We will have plenty when we believe in plenty rather than in lack.*

There wasn't the slightest doubt in Jesus' mind but that there was more than enough to feed all the people. The loaves and fishes were multiplied by His realization of abundance. So complete was His conviction that He gave thanks *before* the actual abundance appeared. The lesson, of course, is that abundance is the result of the richness of our inner attitude. When the inner attitude of realization is strengthened by giving thanks, the results appear automatically.

Thanksgiving is evidence of total acceptance. The loaves and the fishes represent ideas of abundance. Let us follow through with Jesus in the five-step process that resulted in abundance:

1. "He took the seven loaves and the fishes."
   Start with the ideas you have, then get your purpose clearly in mind.
2. "And gave thanks."
   Make your ideas productive and bring your goal to life through realization and completion.
3. "And brake them."
   Do something about it. Use what you have. Organize, arrange, and utilize your powers of accomplishment.
4. "And gave to his disciples."
   The disciples are our twelve basic attitudes. Give everything you have to them and they will do the work for you. They represent creative power working in your mind. The disciples are awakened and activated by your realization and expression of thanksgiving.
5. "And the disciples to the multitude."
   Your disciples, your constructive states of mind, will give your world of affairs and activities (the multitudes) all that is necessary to bring complete success.

Note that these five steps cover the same process that we are developing with our four steps:

1. Thought
2. Feeling
3. Action
4. Acceptance

When a constant attitude of thankfulness is maintained, the inner realization becomes outer fact. Jesus always gave thanks *first*. When He raised Lazarus from the dead, He said, "Father, I thank thee that thou hast heard me. And I knew that thou hearest me always," (John 11:41, 2) and then He gave His command, "Lazarus, come forth," again illustrating the principle that thanksgiving brings realization, and that realization must precede action. When there is complete realization, the action is always successful. Go through the process of inner realization before acting upon anything. Conclude your treatment with the statement, "I give thanks that this is an already accomplished fact in my experience; I await the outcome with perfect confidence."

This attitude of acceptance, gratitude and receptivity is reached, for example, when we say grace before our meals. It is a time-honored custom which has great value, and should be observed by everyone. The value of even the plainest fare is greatly increased when we prepare the mind with thanksgiving. This principle works in everything we do.

At one time I was faced with heavy financial obligations and had no money with which to meet them. I had been "between engagements" as an actor for some time. None of my efforts had produced any results, and anxiety had really set in. I had been learning about principles of constructive thinking through my study of the Science of Mind, and had been learning how to apply them through almost daily appointments with my practitioner, Mrs. Josephine Harden of the First Church of Religious Science in New York. I told her of my problems.

"How much money do you need?" Mrs. Harden asked.

I mentioned a considerable amount.

"Do you believe that you will get it?"

"Of course. I have to."

"Have you ever been in a similar situation before?"

"Yes—several times."

"What happened?"

"Something always came up and the money appeared."

"From where?"

"Various places."

"Did you steal it?"

"Of course not."

"Then how did you get it?"

"I earned it."

"From acting?"

"Yes."

"How did you feel then?"

"Wonderful—relieved—happy."

"And how do you feel now?"

"I've told you. I'm worried sick."

"Why?"

"Look, Mrs. Harden, where is this leading us? You know why. I need money!"

"Do you think worrying is going to help?" she asked.

"Well—no, not exactly."

"Didn't you always get what you needed before?"

"Yes—but—"

"Then why are you worrying?"

"Well—I'm just afraid it won't work out this time."

"Why is this time any different?"

I stopped. My practitioner was making me face myself. "All right, Mrs. Harden. I see. So what do we do now?" I surrendered, exhausted.

"The first thing we are going to do is to stop all of the worrying nonsense," she replied. "Next, you are going to remember how you felt the last time you got a nice engagement and a fat check which solved your money problems. Now think of such a time. Do you remember one?"

"Well, it's been quite a while," I stalled.

"That has nothing to do with it. Come on now, let's get down to business," she insisted. My practitioner was making me get my mind straightened out whether I wanted to or not.

"All right," I answered. "I remember one time when—"

"Good. You don't have to tell me the details. Just think about it for a moment. Get the feeling of it. Remember just how you felt then."

"All right," I agreed as I started to relive that situation of several years ago. I became relaxed and still as I re-created it in my mind. I felt all the relief and exultation which had accompanied the original experience. My practitioner and I worked on this for nearly an hour, and when we had finished I was a completely changed person. My mind was free from worry and I was filled with a warm, expectant feeling. I *knew* that everything was going to be all right. It *was* all right.

Mrs. Harden was doing just what any good practitioner does. She was helping me reverse my thought from negative to positive, so that a new chain of constructive causation was started. During the remainder of our session we completed the steps necessary to bring me to full realization of my good. The following four steps were developed: visualization, feeling, imagination, thanksgiving.

After I had visualized my past moment of triumph and was actually reliving that circumstance, it was a simple matter to transfer my mood to a feeling of expectation and realization concerning my present situation. We were using the technique which I have since taught to thousands of students. It is simply this:

1. *Remember the most wonderful thing that ever happened to you.*
2. *Visualize it fully. Relive every detail of it.*
3. *Develop the inner feeling of how you felt then.*
4. *Imagine the complete and successful working out of what you want to happen now.*
5. *Transfer your feeling of elation and realization to the current situation.*
6. *Give thanks that the whole matter is settled and already satisfactorily worked out.*

Toward the close of our consultation, Mrs. Harden drew the curtains of a large picture window and we stood looking out over fantastic Manhattan.

"What do you see out there?" she inquired.

"Why—New York—," I said.

"Of course. But what do you really see?"

"Just about everything," I mused. "People, buildings, movement—probably more of everything in one place than there is any place else on earth."

"How much do you think it is all worth?"

"Billions, trillions—more than I can imagine."

"How much money did you say you needed?" Mrs. Harden asked.

I laughed. I got the point. How could I have been concerned about lack when there was so much abundance everywhere? I was now looking at things in an entirely different light.

But how did it all work out?

Late that evening I was on a plane for Detroit to play the lead in a commercial film. At the conclusion of the film, which was completed in three days instead of the anticipated six, I was given a check for an amount just double my stipulated salary!

"There must be some mistake," I stammered.

"No. No mistake," the producer answered. "Oh, didn't they tell you? We plan to show this film on television, so rather than bother about it later, we decided to pay everyone the television salary now."

And, believe it or not, the amount on the check was exactly the figure I had mentioned just a few days before when my practitioner had asked how much I needed!

Where had it all come from? Out of my own consciousness, of course. Nothing can happen to you without happening through you. When my mind was changed through scientific prayer treatment work, I changed, and my circumstances changed, too. It is as simple as that. Realization of abundance brings abundance.

You don't believe it? Try it. You say that in my case it was luck, chance, coincidence? There is no such thing as luck. We create our own. And it ceases to be coincidence when it happens more often than not.

Incidentally, this flow of good can often go on and on. I found that out when I returned to New York after this same experience.

First of all, in my mail was my income tax refund which had been held up for some months. This, too, was for an amount which, in itself, would have met my needs. In addition, shortly after my return there came a series of calls which led to a role in a Broadway play, a series of television programs, and a film engagement. You see, the channels opened then, and continue to remain open today.

HOW MANY THINGS DO YOU HAVE TO BE THANKFUL FOR?

Start right now to build the habit of thankfulness. Start by making a list of twenty-five things you are thankful for, and specifically give thanks for each one of them. Take time to visualize each one fully. Get the feeling of it in its full expression. Give your imagination full play. Realize that there is no limit to the good that is expressed through you. Reach the realization that the same power that created all of these good things in your life is an unlimited source from which will flow whatever good you accept. Reach the realization of desired good and give thanks for it even though it has not yet appeared. Give your imagination full play in making this a very real inner experience.

As you give thanks for the original list of twenty-five things, you will be building a foundation of continuous thankfulness. Then let the list expand indefinitely. Thanksgiving is a way of life. Let it release your magnificent potential and bring you the realization of all good things.

Giving Thanks for Good Starts a "Chain Reaction"

The habit of giving thanks starts a chain reaction which is endless. Form the habit of giving thanks for unexpected as well as expected good. Say this treatment over to yourself:

I don't know what is on the way for me but I know it can only be good. I give thanks for all good things in my life whatever they may be and from whatever direction they may come. I set no limits. I am not concerned with where, why, how or when good things happen. I know that God is the source of my supply and everything arrives in proper order. I give thanks for all good things— expected or unexpected. I expect unexpected good today. And so it is.

THE POWER OF SILENCE

An Eastern proverb says, "All things proceed from the quiet mind." We align ourselves with the source of all power by simply being still. "Be still and know that I am God," sings the psalmist. Only in the silence can we reach full realization. As the human mind is still, Divine Mind takes over. Make it a habit to sit in relaxed and complete silence several times each day. This will recharge your spiritual batteries and give you renewed power and energy.

Just be still and know that all good is taking place through you. Don't merely *try* to be still; *be* still. Do nothing; soon a deep sense of peace will flow through you. You will realize the presence of God indwelling.

Here is your Daily Guide to realization:

DAILY GUIDE TO REALIZATION

I give thanks for the realization of who and what I really am. I give thanks for the beauty and wonder of life. I realize that there is no limit to my achievement and experience. I have unlimited possibilities. I have infinite potential. Today I realize what a privilege it is to be alive. I realize that I am on the pathway to perfection and I am growing every step along the way.

Thought, feeling, action and acceptance give me the realization of my greatest good. There is no place I cannot go, nothing I cannot do, and no limit to what I can become as I realize the magnificence of my inner potential. My mind is filled with noble thoughts. My heart is filled with deep and loving response. I act intelligently and powerfully to bring greater good into my world. I accept all the abundance which life has to offer and I spread love and good will throughout my world. I am attuned to that which is greater than I, and I give it an outlet through all that I do. I have a deep realization of inner peace as I get my life in order. Spirit, mind and body are in perfect balance in me and I am attuned to harmony and order at all times.

I am a happy person. I am cheerful and pleasant at all times. I enjoy life and I make the lives of others more enjoyable. I experience happiness and I express it at all times. I realize the joy of making others happy.

I am healthy in mind, emotion and body. I am made whole as I get myself out of the way and let the divine circuits come through. I am thankful for being a whole person. Prosperity and success are realized as I cooperate with the creative process in bringing all good things into my life and into the lives of others.

Wisdom and understanding grow out of my inner realization of life and love. I know that God is within me and I am made in His image and likeness. I know that I am perfect even as God in Heaven is perfect. I experience the fullness of life on every level. I embrace the realization of the Greater Self. I attain complete realization now. And so it is.

11

❖ ❖ ❖

On the Threshold of Great Experience

The principles and techniques of this book are developed for the purpose of helping us get in the driver's seat and stay there. We alone are responsible for the experiences which we have. The outer experience comes from the inner state of mind. When we learn to think straight and control our feelings and reactions, we cannot help being in the driver's seat.

"Mommy," a little girl I knew once observed, "today is much happier than yesterday."

"Why is that, dear?"

"Because yesterday my thoughts pushed me around, but today I'm pushing *them* around."

That's about it. It is all a matter of who is taking whom for a ride.

"Where are you going with the big dog?" a man once asked a small boy.

"I don't know exactly," panted the boy as he was tugged along. "I'm just waiting to find out where he wants to go, and then I'm going to take him there!"

The Jet Propulsion Principle in Balanced Creating Power

Similarly, life is like having a tiger by the tail, until we learn how to control and harness for constructive purposes the tremendous power within us. The relationship is something like two-way jet propulsion. Our feelings project us into whatever we do; we project our feelings into everything we do. Our purpose here is to develop a balanced conditioning of the subconscious mind so that the conscious mind is in complete control of the inner power at all times. We want to be able to choose where we are going and what we are going to do, and we want to control the attitudes with which we do it.

Our inner attitudes and feelings provide the power drive for accomplishment. They provide our motive power. They move us and we can learn to move them in the direction we want to go. Too little emotion leaves us negative and ineffectual; too much throws us out of control. Feeling is the secret of power and a balanced relationship to life, but it must be controlled feeling.

Our feelings project into our world through our actions and relationships as clearly as if we announced them with loudspeakers and neon signs. This intensity generates a tremendous potential of usable energy. That is their purpose. That is why we have devoted the first ten chapters to their development. Now we must learn how to use them effectively for accomplishing what we want to accomplish and in becoming the person we want to be.

However, this inner head of steam must be released and utilized constructively, or it will destroy us. Misdirected energy results in frenetic, busy turbulence that hinders true accomplishment. Unused energy produces frustrations and pressures which wear away at the body and interfere with purposeful action. We simply must learn how to utilize our inner atomic power so as to get the greatest results, and achieve happiness and the rich, full life at the same time.

Projecting Your "Subliminal Signs" Effectively

What are you projecting right now? Are you registering the impression you want to give? Are you in control of yourself and all situations? Are you sure of yourself? Do you express authority? Do people have confidence in you? Are you clicking in life, or are you missing the boat? Be honest with yourself and measure the results you are achieving against your true potential. If you are falling short, there is a reason. Let's find out what it is.

The late Lew Sarett, professor of Professional Speech at Northwestern University, from whom I received a good part of my early training, taught that the impressions we give and the effectiveness we achieve are due largely to "subliminal signs." These, he said, we are not aware of projecting and the listener or observer is not necessarily aware of receiving, but they register nevertheless.

For example, we often "feel" a certain way about a particular person even though we can't explain why. This is intuition, direct knowing without conscious thought. Intuition is largely the result of forming impressions from these "subliminal signs" without being aware that we are doing so. The image we project is really the result of everything we think, feel, say and do. If any of these are out of focus, the outer picture will be distorted. An uncertain movement, a nervous mannerism, the expression of the eyes and face, the tone of voice, the position and movement of the body, are all subliminal signs which project the picture of what we are. Our job is to develop and control what we are. The projection is automatic.

Think of it as being like film running through a motion picture projector:

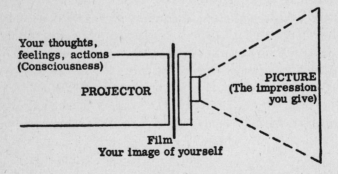

The "film" is what you really are. The "projector" is made up of your thoughts, feelings and actions. The "picture" is the result of what you really are, conditioned and projected by your thoughts, feelings and actions. Naturally, the picture will be right when the film and the projector are in order.

The first factor is the film. No matter how hard we try we will never get a super "A" spectacle out of "B" or "C" film. We can only project what we are. Therefore, if we want to change the outer picture, we must change the film that we run through the projector—ourselves. Of course, we must keep this inner self in good order; blurred or twisted film cannot give a good picture. We must also see that we have a good, serviceable projector with which to show the film. The equipment must be serviceable, the light bright, clear and powerful, and the film must be properly threaded. When everything is right on the projection end, what we show and accomplish on the screen of experience will be a true projection of what we are at this particular stage of our development.

Of course, we can always improve the quality of our film and we can develop a new and more powerful projector. This is exactly what happens when we apply sound scientific mental and spiritual principles to our lives. All this work is done within ourselves, upon the film and the projector. We use the outer picture to gauge the focus and clarity of our inner imaging and projecting equipment.

How Effective Is Your Part in the "Theatre of Life"?

Life is like a play—in a way, *it is a play*. As Shakespeare wrote: "All the world's a stage, and all the men and women merely players. They have their exits and their entrances and each man in his time plays many parts. . . ."

Which part are you playing on the stage of life? What character are you portraying? What action are you projecting? What mood are you sustaining? Are you a leading man or woman, a character actor, a villain, or a bit player? Are you playing out your drama in front of beautiful scenery, or are your surroundings drab and uninteresting? Is yours a cheerful and happy production with beautiful lights, costumes and music; or is it a dull, talky piece?

In the theatre of life each of us "plays many parts." In our lives, each of us is playwright, director, scene designer and actor. God is the great impresario—the producer.

As the playwright, we do the choosing, planning and developing of our life's play. We deal with beliefs, convictions and ideas. We use thought, imagination and intuition in formulating the theme and meaning of our existence. We plot the action, choose the characters, and picture the incidents necessary to tell our story. The playwright within us must do his work or there is no play. Without a play there can be no production. Without thought, planning and action there can be no experience. Without experience there is no life. God is the great potential from which all things flow. The playwright within us chooses and plans what part of that potential is to be expressed at any particular time.

The director within us has a vital job as one of our creative faculties. The director interprets, plans and coordinates the entire production. He directs. He has absolute authority over what is to be done and how it is to be done. What direction are you giving to your life? What kind of job are you doing in coordinating things? A purposeful life must have sound direction, planning, and coordination. We must learn to use wisely and efficiently the various elements we have to work with.

Both the playwright and director represent the conscious mind in thought, choice, planning and judgment, but they are also the subconscious faculties of memory, imagination, intuition and feeling. Each of our faculties is part of every other one. They must work hand in hand.

The scene designer is also an integral part of the whole creative team. He provides the background against which the action is to take place. The designer helps to set the mood and project the entire picture by the use of locale, form, perspective, color and light. The designer also uses both the objective and subjective faculties in his creative work. Each department is an integral part of the total production. We must be balanced, integrated and unified if we are to make a success of life. The playwright, the director, the scene designer, and the actor must all work together within us under the inspiration and guidance of the producer—the creative Spirit and Law.

All of this preparation and planning comes to life through the actor. He must project visually, audibly, and through action, what the others had in mind, giving it warmth and excitement through his own creative genius. The inspiration of the producer, the intention of the playwright, the interpretation of the director, the mood of the designer, are all projected through the performance of the actor.

In addition, the actor has the responsibility of presenting the work of all the others. If their work has been good and his is good, the play is a success. If their work has been good and his is bad, it has all been for nothing. It is the acting which is seen. Very few plays can survive bad acting. Very few lives can be successful if they are portrayed in bad actions and unworthy deeds. The results which are seen are the factors upon which we are judged. We are judged by performance.

In the theatre, plays are often turned from failures into successes by constant rehearsal and changes during extended tryout tours, during which the play is performed to see how it goes in front of audiences "on the road" before it is brought into New York. This often entails a complete rewriting, redirecting, redesigning, and recasting of the entire production. Nothing matters except perfecting the production. This often requires the replacement of various people connected with it. There is a good deal of trial and error involved, just as there is in all of life; but there is also a good deal of discipline and hard work, just as there must be in life if we are to be successful.

The qualities that go to make up a good production in the theatre are the same ones that go to make up a good person. Just as the playwright, director, designer, and actor are all vital to the whole production of a play, so the aspects that they represent are essential to the projection of the entire person and the balanced life.

Our twelve basic steps are the tools of the professional theatre worker, just as they are our basic equipment in the drama of life. When these inner attributes of the mind are completely developed and balanced, the results cannot help but be successful. When we neglect any of them the results will be incomplete and unsatisfactory. We must work constantly to perfect the whole production—the whole person.

Imagination and feeling are essential in the theatre just as they are in life, but they must be organized, controlled and used wisely. These subjective powers must be disciplined by our conscious faculties. Thought plus feeling produces action, but thought must come first. Planning, choice, and discipline are important aspects of the conscious mind.

The beginning of the rehearsal period of a play is one of planning, working out, explaining, choosing and formulating thoughts about the job in hand. Good directors will be so thoroughly prepared that they have the entire production laid out in their minds. They will know what to do and how to do it, but their plans are flexible enough to take advantage of the contributions of others.

As the rehearsals progress, a definite pattern of action is set. The actors learn their lines, their stage business, their movements, their cues for exits and entrances, and all the hundred and one things necessary to the play. As they are learning the outer words and actions, the actors are at the same time building the characters from within with their thought, feeling and imagination. It is not enough just to act like the character; the actor must become the character.

This explains the whole difference between failure and success on the stage just as it does in life. It is a matter of going all the way. The conscious and subconscious functions of the mind must be in perfect accord. This is accomplished during the rehearsal period of the play. In life, too, we have our rehearsal periods—of thought, planning, prayer, and meditation. Workers in the theatre learn their business and how to get the desired result. In the great play of life we must work to become similarly adept.

Since the business of the theatre is the representation of life, the rehearsal period is one of learning how to apply the creative process so that the eventual performance will unfold creditably. The rehearsal period is one of learning. Once the technical process of learning is accomplished, the actors start to project subconsciously and the play comes to life.

We are all actors. We are constantly projecting what we are onto our world stage. Some of us are performing failure, unhappiness and illness, while others are effortlessly and joyously projecting success, happiness and health. These things do not come about by accident. It is all a matter of what we have rehearsed in our minds. The prevailing mental attitude determines what appears in our experience.

Therefore, our job now is to choose and form our inner images, concepts and attitudes and to rehearse them until they become so completely ingrained in our consciousness that it is impossible for us to act otherwise. As we learn to do this we will constantly give exciting and successful performances in all that we do.

The Golden Bridge—What It Is and How to Use It

I have developed a technique of life rehearsal that I call the "Golden Bridge." The Golden Bridge is the actual completion of our inner identification with the creative process. As we build the bridge in our minds we are constructing a path upon which we travel to completion and accomplishment. The Golden Bridge is a rehearsal for life. By this process we form the invisible structure upon which is built the formation of our lives. It defines where we are going and provides a means for getting there. The Golden Bridge utilizes all of our creative faculties. It takes chance and effort out of our activities. It dissolves the barriers of time and space by building within us an awareness of purpose and completion. The use of the Golden Bridge will enable us to transcend our human failings and weaknesses, and will lift us into a consciousness of our true place in the great scheme of things.

The Golden Bridge will release the power of your magnificent potential, and give you the necessary direction for complete fulfillment. The Golden Bridge has become for me life's most valuable tool. It is a device for bringing divine power into tangible expression. It is tremendous. Let's learn to use it.

Become completely relaxed. Detach your mind from all concerns and random thoughts. Use the techniques and Guides to Life discussed in this book to enable you to do this. Remove all personal effort as you become still and identify yourself with the Indwelling Reality. Visualize light and inner peace and beauty, and let the feeling of power and strength generate within you.

Let yourself become filled with the spiritual fuel which provides the thrust to project you into new and vital experience. Take time to get completely quiet inside. Form the picture of yourself as a whole person—spirit, mind and body. As you achieve this feeling of completeness you will be ready to build and travel the magic span of the Golden Bridge.

Picture yourself as a magnificent and powerful rocket which is being projected along a beautifully arching trajectory into new spheres of understanding and experience. We span the infinite realms of experience as we traverse the Golden Bridge. We start from where we are. What we are doing in inner visualization looks something like this:

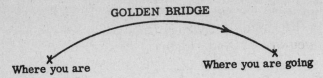

GOLDEN BRIDGE

Where you are   Where you are going

The Golden Bridge is the upper path of spirit, mind and imagination. It enables us to reach our destination by rising above the obstacles of ignorance, mistakes and trial-and-error experience which block our way when we fail to use the power within us.

Jesus said, "I go to prepare a place for you." (John 14:2-4) The "I" is your inner creative awareness. Visualization, imagination and realization are its natural capacities. You are this "I." Send it ahead of you and let it prepare the place for you. Identify yourself with it completely in the inner stillness and you will go with it into the glorious realms to which it will lead you. Trust it completely. It is intuition inspired by spiritual realization. It is your real self. Through it you build the Golden Bridge of your life.

This technique may be applied to any section of your experience no matter how small it may be—from a single moment to eternity. The Golden Bridge enables us to know where we are going, because after we have once spanned it in our inner consciousness, we then return and travel it in the action of experience without any peril of losing our way.

Do you see how it works? When the inner consciousness once reaches the destination—even though the outer self may still need to go through plans, problems and worldly actions—the inner self has already reached its destination and achieved its goal. It is a matter of reaching absolute conviction. There is no better way to convince ourselves that we can do a thing than actually to do it. When we travel the Golden Bridge we arrive at our destination first as preparation for starting to go.

Suppose you were to take a trip to a distant country where you have never been. You would arrange the trip with your travel agent, who would help you make plans and would tell you what you would expect along the way and after you got there. You would study travel folders, and learn the language and customs of the place you are to visit. You would provide yourself with tickets and the necessary items to take on the trip. You would make all arrangements. You would prepare yourself completely for a pleasant journey. In essence, you would take the trip many times vicariously before you actually started on the physical journey. You would *be* there in consciousness long before you ever left home.

So it is with the Golden Bridge. But it is more than just an imaginary journey. It is complete preparation for what is to follow. We both misunderstand and underestimate the true function and power of the imagination. We are what and where we are because we have first imagined it, consciously or subconsciously. The Golden Bridge speeds up the process and makes it easier. The Golden Bridge is the *direct* path. It avoids the detours, the twistings and turnings, and the pain and suffering, the misdirections, the discouragements, and the lost ways. The Golden Bridge looks something like this:

Visualize the Golden Bridge as leading straight up to the summit of a high mountain, which is also traversed by a winding, twisting road. The mountain represents the achievement and enlightenment attained through growth and experience. It represents the distance we travel as we keep moving upward. It may, and undoubtedly does, take many lifetimes to reach the top of the mountain. But the important thing to remember is: *We all make it eventually.* The Golden Bridge enables us to progress more surely and more rapidly by developing our full inner resources. None of us really knows how far he has progressed up the mountain. We do know that we are on our way upward, and our challenge is to go as far as we can.

The winding road up the mountain represents the long and slow trek upward through experience, trial and error, toil and suffering. It reaches the summit too, but the trip is a long and perilous one, filled with many turnings, backtrackings and detours.

This visual presentation of the Golden Bridge should be firmly fixed in your mind as a master symbol for meditation and inner spiritual work. Even though we may get confused and lost in dealing with life's problems, we can always get back on the right track by visualizing this straight path. We can never get lost when we stay on the Golden Bridge.

The Golden Bridge is a means of cooperating with the creative Law of life. It enables us to use the power within us for the real business of life—growth and accomplishment on every level. It enables us to flow with the tide, the inner resurgence of energy and power which is always seeking expression. The Golden Bridge is one means of making our personal will one with the Divine Will. Anything worthwhile must be an expression of Divine Will. Constant inner work will enable us to discover what this Will is and will enable us to cooperate with it. An awareness of the larger picture gives meaning and purpose to the adventure of living.

This book is a projection of the Golden Bridge, and each of the twelve basic attitudes are steps along the way. We will move constantly upward when we apply and strengthen them. The twelve attitudes are characteristics of the Higher Self, and the journey of life is for the purpose of attaining identification with it. Let's learn to use the Golden Bridge as the path along which we walk hand in hand with our inner partner—the Higher Self.

The Golden Bridge technique may be used to prepare the way for any segment of activity or experience—an hour, a day, a week, a month, a year, or a lifetime. Start by using it to span each day. Mentally cut through any doubts and anticipated difficulties until the path of the day is projected straight and true before you. In this way you arrive mentally at your destination before you actually start the trip.

You have no idea of the freedom and ease with which you travel once you have learned to do this. It will give you the direction and the certainty which will enable you to meet every situation with confidence and power. Once you *know* everything is going to be all right—the conviction which you build with your Golden Bridge—you will not be concerned with minor difficulties which may arise. The very fact that you have built your conviction in itself projects an authority and power which keeps difficulties from arising, and causes everything to work out properly.

Golden Bridge for This Day

Construct your Golden Bridge for each day as soon as possible upon awakening. Get perfectly still and travel step by step to the end of the day, progressively building the conviction that you are actually there doing the things which you are visualizing and stating, and that they are completed. Make your statements aloud if possible, for this will keep your mind on a straight track and build a stronger inner feeling.

Here is a model for a Golden Bridge for one day. Adapt it to your own situation.

I am now building the Golden Bridge of this day. I give thanks for this day and the potential of great experience during every moment of it. Throughout this day I am guided and directed by the Inner Intelligence which prepares the way for me and makes straight and true the pathway of my experience.

Everything I do has purpose and meaning. I work efficiently and well. I am in perfect control of myself and every situation at all times. I am free from all doubt and uncertainty as I move serenely ahead. I put my best foot forward at all times. I know that what I plan to do is already an accomplished fact in my experience, and every outer action is a projection of this inner pattern. In this way I can make no mistakes, because I have already traveled the road which I am on. Being sure of myself, I am able to adapt successfully to any unexpected situation which may arise. I handle everything as it arises, being already sure of the outcome. I live joyously, eagerly and expectantly all day long. I love life and I love to live.

Each second of time moves me that much closer to the completion of a happy and successful day. I easily complete my preparations for this day of success. Everything in my home and family is harmonious and orderly. Love and goodwill bless my relations with my family and all other people throughout this day. I am kind, understanding, and courteous at all times.

Breakfast this morning is a leisurely and pleasurable experience. Good conversation and sharing of viewpoints grace our table. My family and I are nourished in soul as well as in body. Everything is wonderful.

I am protected and guided as I journey to my office. I enjoy the trip. I eagerly anticipate the work which awaits me there. I am on time for every appointment, and everything is accomplished successfully and is arranged according to the best interests of everyone concerned. What I do, I do well. My work is thorough and of high quality. I constantly work to improve myself and what I do. I am a top-rate person. I do a good job of being my best self at all times. I take joy in the doing, and I let results and rewards take care of themselves. I am free from concern, worry or fatigue. I gather energy and momentum as I go along. I operate as a whole person. I get the most out of life today and always. There is no limit to my potential. I am on the high road at all times. I am a success in every way.

Continue in this way until you have covered your entire day. Give special attention to important appointments, decisions and projects. Take the affirmative approach, and keep at it until the picture is clear and your conviction is strong. Cover everything, no matter how large or how small. The results which you achieve depend upon the thoroughness of your inner mental work. Refuse to let your mind dwell upon anything except what you want it to accept.

Spend approximately a half hour building your Golden Bridge at the beginning of each day. Be thorough about it, and give it full time.

Doing so will add immeasurably to your efficiency and accomplishment. Once you form the habit of building the Golden Bridge you will never try to do anything without it. The longer you work with this technique, the more efficient you will become, and the easier it will be to do. As you do your inner job well, you will be able to handle anything that comes up without it throwing you.

Then, too, there are times during the day when you will need to become quiet and do some repair work in the Golden Bridge, or you may need to alter the original design. Don't let this upset you; just do it. Ride with life, be flexible and adaptable, but always work from a solid inner structure. Nothing is more important than this. The Golden Bridge is of inestimable value in this respect.

Having completed your Golden Bridge for the day, or any particular segment thereof, release it—forget about it, and go ahead and do what you have to do. The structure is there, and will automatically provide the pattern for the action which follows. You will be amazed by the results you achieve, and how much more enjoyable life becomes.

I use the Golden Bridge in everything I do. It has been of particular help in presenting my lectures. After thorough study and preparation of my material, I mentally build the Golden Bridge, visualizing myself delivering my talk, seeing the audience receiving it—every step through to the conclusion. Then I forget all about it. As far as I am personally concerned, it is a completed fact in my experience. The work is completed. There just remains the pleasure of performance. Just before going on the platform I am completely quiet for an hour, unifying my consciousness with inner guidance; then I go out and have a good time. The success of the presentation depends upon the thoroughness of this inner work. If you are a speaker, I heartily recommend this procedure. It will free you from the necessity of notes, and will remove all tension and nervousness; it will give you a never-ending supply of worthwhile things to say, and will enable you to say them effectively; it will form a powerful inner bond between you and your audience, and it will give you more freedom, enjoyment and success than you had ever thought possible.

The Need of Retracing Your Steps on the Golden Bridge

A technique of retrospection goes hand in hand with the Golden Bridge. Let us suppose that you have built your Golden Bridge and have traveled it—successfully or unsuccessfully—throughout the day. You are now back in bed, where you awakened to start your day many hours before. No matter what the day has been like, get quiet inside and deliberately go back over the Golden Bridge of your day in reverse order. Start from where you are, and retrace your steps through the evening, at dinner, the afternoon, lunch, morning and all the way back to when you awakened. Fix everything so that it is right. Forgive yourself and others. If you were wrong, admit it.

If a situation was handled badly, correct it in your mind and rehearse it visually, with thought, word, action and feeling, until it is right. Erase all unpleasant memories, impressions and confusions and replace them with the corrected ones. Your subconscious mind will retain what you instruct it to retain. Correct your mistakes and fix things that went wrong, giving particular attention to your thoughts and attitudes and what you said and felt. This is exactly what the director does after a rehearsal, or after a performance which needs improving.

As you do this you will cleanse your mind, your memory, and your emotional state of everything except what you want to remain there as a permanent and constructive part of your consciousness. You will balance the mental, emotional and spiritual budget. You will sleep better than you ever slept in your life and you will awaken refreshed and strengthened. Remember, the feeling you go to sleep with is the one you wake up with. When your mind is free as you go to sleep, powerful subconscious natural forces are free to work through you, refreshing and instructing your mind, developing your soul, and rebuilding your body.

There are no more valuable life tools than the Golden Bridge and its counterpart, the process of retrospection, by which you go back over the events of your day in reverse order. When you practice these disciplines faithfully you will rebuild your life completely. You will experience health, happiness, success and fulfillment because you will be constantly projecting them mentally, emotionally and spiritually into your world.

DAILY GUIDE TO PROJECTION

I project a consciousness of success and right action into my world. I send my Higher Self before me, preparing the way for full and beautiful experience. I clear my mind of everything unlike the nature of good. I fill myself with powerful spiritual fuel which projects me into an orbit of ever-expanding experience. I attune myself to peace, order and right action.

I form the pattern of perfect experience by rounding out my inner life. I correct all mistakes before they happen. I examine my every thought and feeling, bringing them into line with the good, the true and the beautiful. I become the person I would like to be by knowing that I am that person. As I live well inwardly, I project an outer life which is noble and fine. I know that what I think and feel constantly shows. I am a living advertisement of the contents of my mind. I entertain only those ideas and attitudes by which I am willing to be known.

I move serenely forward into the adventure of life today. I am filled with inspiration and enthusiasm. I am guided and protected by the Infinite Intelligence. I express this Intelligence in everything I say and do. I project confidence and authority. I am sure of myself in every situation. I am filled with the strength and energy to be what I am and to do what I have to do. I am a vehicle propelled by the motor of understanding and love. I am moved by powerful forces.

I am an individual projection of life in action. God is expressed through me at the point where I am. God is love. I project love. God is peace. I am at peace. God is beauty. My life expresses balance and order. God is power. I am strong. God is infinite. I am free from all limitation. God is truth. I grow in wisdom and understanding. God is One. I am a well-integrated and unified individual. I am God in action at the level of my understanding. I project my Divine Heritage today. And so it is.

12

❖ ❖ ❖

Get Out and Get Going

"What is the secret of your success?" someone asked the late eminent scientist, Dr. George Washington Carver.

"I pray as if everything depends upon God," he replied. "Then I work as if everything depends upon me."

Dr. Carver understood the place and importance of action in the creative process.

In Chapter 7 we started developing four main points toward achievement—thought, feeling, action, release. In the last chapter we talked about inner action. Now we are talking about outer action—working and doing.

First we get an idea. Then we develop it inwardly through treatment and prayer—building right mental and emotional attitudes toward it. This gives it clarity, energy and power. Then comes the time to move—to put the creative machinery into action. It is time for the performance of the play we have been rehearsing. We are ready to "try out" in front of an actual audience. The "dry runs" are over. This is the real thing.

Throughout this book we have been talking about what to do and how to do it. Now it is time to apply the new ideas and techniques through intelligently directed action.

Yes, there always comes the time when we must act. Self-expression is essential in life. Self-preservation depends upon it. The inner dynamic must be put to work. It is much like heating water in a boiler: a head of steam is developed and power is available to be used. In our personal application, interest, desire and intention are developed through scientifically directed thought, or prayer treatment. This is the flame which heats up the inner power. Once we get our head of steam up in this way we must act or else blow up. Action is the outlet for the energy of life.

Once a young lady came to a minister I know for counseling and prayer upon a very important human problem. She wanted a husband, but she was having difficulty meeting the right man—in fact, any man.

"There *is* the one right man for you," the minister counseled. "One who needs you as much as you need him."

"Where is he?" demanded the girl. "How do I find him?"

"By becoming the kind of woman who will automatically attract the kind of man you want in your life," replied the minister.

"How do I do that?" pressed the young lady. "How do I become this kind of person?"

The minister explained to the young woman how to build a true image of herself with directed thought and imagination through the proper use of prayer treatment. He also showed her how to build a mental equivalent of her husband-to-be through the same means. It was our basic principle applied to this very human situation. It can be applied to any circumstance involving acquisition, achievement or accomplishment. It has two parts:

1. Get clearly in mind what you want.
2. Become that thing in your mind.

The minister's telephone awakened him late on the Saturday night following the interview.

"He hasn't appeared yet," the voice of the young lady reprimanded.

"Who hasn't appeared?" the minister muttered sleepily.

"My man," the young lady continued. "Remember you said if I followed what you said, the right man would appear in my life? Well—where is he?"

"Where are you?" the minister asked.

"In my room doing what you said—treating to become the kind of woman who will attract the kind of man I want in my life. But nothing has happened, and I want to know why," she answered.

"Where is your roommate this evening?" the minister asked.

"Oh, she's at a party at a friend's apartment down the hall."

"Weren't you invited?"

"Oh, yes, but I thought I'd better stay home and do my treatment work for a husband."

"Are there men at the party?" the minister asked.

"Oh, yes."

"Now, look, young lady," said the minister, "you've prayed enough for awhile. You put on your prettiest dress and go down there to that party where the men are."

"But I don't understand. You said—"

"I said to visualize yourself becoming the kind of person who would attract the kind of man you wanted in your life. I didn't say he would fly in through the window. Now you get on to that party!"

Shortly afterward, the young lady did find her husband, but only after she followed her prayer by going out to meet him. Outer action must follow inner action if we are to get results.

Get Out and Get Going:

You will note that in the many treatments and in the Guides to Life at the end of each of our chapters, we frequently affirm "perfect order and right action." As we establish order in our inner thoughts and attitudes, right action follows automatically.

The equation looks like this:

Thought + Feeling + Action = Completion.

The sequence is always the same. When we supply the three ingredients of the formula, results are automatic.

During my twenty years as an actor I frequently found myself "between engagements," as most actors do. These are the most difficult times of an actor's life. The contrast between the intensely exciting and active periods of employment and the following periods of inactivity are hard to adjust to. There is nothing more destructive than having too much time on your hands and nothing to do with it.

When the suffering of inactivity became too intense, I used to turn my attention to writing, for which I have harbored an ambition since childhood. When my next engagement was not forthcoming, I used to get started on a writing project. It never failed—just as I was getting under way, a call would come from my agent or one of the studios, and I would go to work as an actor. *Action produces action.* Constructive action, inner and outer, produces constructive results in accord with your inner desires.

The principle of circulation is involved, too. Just as the young lady of our story couldn't find a husband while sitting alone in her room, so you and I are not likely to enjoy life's rewards when we remain withdrawn from life. Untold numbers of good things have come to me simply because I have been in the right place at the right time—where things are happening. The mainstream of life is always moving, and it flows through us when we get into the swim of things. Learn to build your life inwardly through the procedures we are discussing here, but know that this must be followed by doing something about it.

Action, of course, entails decision. We must make a choice, work out an intelligent plan of action, and stick to it. This takes purpose and courage, but when the inner conviction is coupled with sustained action, results are always forthcoming.

Following several years of hard work, combining acting in Hollywood with the building of our ministry in Santa Barbara, I began to feel the need for a larger field of action. I felt that greater results could be achieved if I combined my two major activities into a single plan of action. I felt that I was ready to do something bigger in the ministry, but my work in motion pictures and television kept getting in the way. Finally, I made a decision—one of the most important of my life.

I had made a commitment to speak at the large summer conference of the Churches of Religious Science at Asilomar on the Monterey Peninsula. I eagerly accepted this honor, and my wife and I made plans to spend an entire week in meditation and study in the spiritual atmosphere of the conference. No sooner had we arrived at Asilomar, however, than I received a telephone call from Hollywood with the offer of a television series which would have brought me many thousands of dollars.

"I'll call you back," I told my agent on the long-distance telephone. "I'll have to let you know."

"What do you mean—you'll call me back!" my agent exploded. "This is the best thing that's ever come your way. Now get on a plane and get down here. They need you the first thing tomorrow morning."

"I'll have to decide first," I answered. "I'll call you back." I hung up with the agent still sputtering on the telephone. I stood there for a moment, dazed and uncertain. It wasn't the first time I had been faced with a decision of this kind. But this time I felt intuitively—I couldn't explain why—that the showdown was for bigger stakes than I had ever played for before. I wanted to accept the Hollywood offer, but it would have meant disrupting plans and inconveniencing a lot of people. I had ridden two horses for a long time, but now I needed to choose between them.

My wife and I talked it over when I got back to our cottage. She looked at me for a long time and finally asked, "Do you really have a choice?" Silently we walked down the beach and sat looking out at the breakers coming in for over an hour, treating upon the issue involved.

Finally, the answer came—the only possible one—and I went to the telephone. I told my exasperated agent to forget the whole thing. My acting career was over—just like that. I turned my back on an activity in which I had been engaged for twenty years—by an act of the will. I had made my choice.

During the remainder of the week, in addition to speaking, I immersed myself in quiet, inner spiritual experience. My conviction steadily grew that I had made the right decision. At the same time, I was preparing for the intensive action that I somehow knew was on the way, although I didn't know what it was to be.

I soon found out. Shortly after my return to Santa Barbara, the telephone rang in my study one afternoon. It was Dr. Ernest Holmes, dean and founder of the Church of Religious Science in Los Angeles.

"How soon can you come down to Los Angeles?" he asked. "Something has turned up that I think you would be interested in."

I was on my way within the hour. Little did I know what was ahead for me. Dr. Frederick Bailes, founder and director of the large independent Science of Mind Church, had decided to retire and devote himself to writing and lecturing; he had asked Dr. Holmes to recommend someone to take over as minister-director, with the understanding that the Science of Mind Church would become an affiliated member of the Church of Religious Science.

"I heard you speak at Asilomar," Dr. Holmes said. "And I think you're ready. It's a tremendous job, but I know you can handle it. Do you want to give it a try?"

"Do you mean you want me to be the minister of the Science of Mind Church?" I could hardly believe my ears.

Ever since I had been in the work, Dr. Frederic Bailes and the Science of Mind Church had represented to me the very top of the metaphysical field. Over the years Dr. Bailes had built the Science of Mind Church into the largest such congregation in the world. And now I was being asked to take his place! I had been overwhelmed when he had once asked me to speak for him on a Sunday morning; but I had never dreamed of anything like this!

"Well, what do you say?" Dr. Holmes asked. "Do you want it?"

"Yes, I want it," I answered. "When do I start?"

"Right away," Dr. Holmes stated.

"Right away—but I do want to talk to Bernice first—and we'll need to get someone to take over in Santa Barbara."

"I have someone to do that," Dr. Holmes continued. "You talk it over with Bernice and let me know."

I did, and there followed a period of intense activity that has never lessened during the years which have followed. Naturally, there have been many problems in conducting this large organization, but everything has always worked out all right. The move brought about many changes in our lives, of course. It meant giving up the home which we had built, and making the change from the quiet of Santa Barbara to the busy bustle of Los Angeles, but we managed it.

I believe that we would never have been able to assume these responsibilities without the stabilizing and strengthening influence of the type of thinking we are talking about in this book. This is one reason why I know that what I am talking about here really works.

We can all be divinely guided if we want to be. There is no chance or luck. Everything is a sequence of cause and effect. What we do inside ourselves produces what happens outside in our world of experience. Never skip your inner work upon yourself; keep bringing your thoughts, attitudes and feelings into order so that right action may follow. The more intensive the outer pressures and responsibilities, the more need there is for inner stabilization. We all have a tendency to skip the quiet inner bolstering when we get swept up in outer activities. There never seems to be enough time—and there will never be unless we take it. We keep every other date, but we take all kinds of liberties with our appointments with ourselves.

Take time to think, to plan, to repair and maintain your inner consciousness. Remember, 90% of your power and effectiveness comes from what you know and what you are, and only 10% from what you actually do. Most people spend little if any time with the inner life; nearly everything is outer activity. This is completely wrong and can only end up in disaster, disease, fatigue and failure. All these result from the failure to maintain the proper balance between inner consciousness and outer activity.

How much time should be spent in spiritual and mental disciplines—prayer, treatment, meditation? This varies somewhat with individuals, but start with the principle of the tithe—10%. The principle of giving 10% of one's income back to God by supporting a spiritual work has enriched everyone who ever practiced it. So has the principle of giving 10% of one's time to God through meditation and prayer.

The Value of Concentrated Prayer

There are 1,440 minutes in a day. Ten percent is 144 minutes to be spent in quiet inner personal work—two hours and twenty-four minutes. It may seem a lot, but once you do it, you will find it the most productive activity in which you have ever engaged. Use this book as your guide. Practice the techniques and go over the guides given at the end of each chapter. Get the basic attitudes so firmly implanted in your mind that you couldn't deviate from them even if you wanted to.

Following this thinking, then, set aside a definite period of time each morning and evening just for your inner spiritual treatment work. Be alone with yourself. Straighten out your thoughts and feelings. Relate yourself to the indwelling power by building constructive attitudes. Speak your affirmations out loud definitely and with conviction. Don't be afraid to do this. It is strictly a matter between you and God. It concerns no one else, so don't be embarrassed. It is true that the hardest person to face is yourself, but once you start to do it regularly, you will be amazed by what it does for you. It will help you get yourself out of the way so the real Self can come through.

It is also a good idea to spend regular periods in treatment and prayer with people who are close to you. This gives a mutual focus for action. Husbands and wives find that the marriage, the family, and the home are strengthened by regular discussion of mutual issues, followed by periods of treatment and prayer.

For years, Bernice and I spent a regular period each day in this shared inner experience. All good things which we experienced or accomplished together grew out of these periods. We simply sat down together, discussed briefly plans for development and action, then after a period of silence we would repeat some affirmations or a well-known prayer such as the Lord's Prayer or the Twenty-Third Psalm. Then we would each in turn make statements of affirmation, conviction and realization about various matters we are dealing with. Finally, we would end the period by giving thanks that right action was already accomplished and that we were guided and directed in all that we did.

If we had plans ahead, we brought them into the prayer treatment, too. If something had gone wrong, we corrected it then and there in our own consciousness. If personal faults had shown up, or if something was not working out, we dealt with these matters in the same way. We have built our lives on this principle, and whatever we have accomplished together personally and professionally is attributable to it.

You can do the same thing. Start right now, and never neglect this important part of your life. It is really very simple. It just takes time and discipline, the components of any action. Use this principle of shared inner experience with the people with whom you work. Make it a habit to start each work day with a period of treatment or prayer. You don't have to make a big religious formality out of it. Remember, religion is something to live by—basically common sense. It is only common sense and good business to get right inside before attempting anything outside. The great Power which is God hears us and responds to us no matter what we say or do. Just make sure that the words of your mouth and the meditations of your heart state what you want to experience. Remember, your every thought and feeling is your prayer. And—make it a good one.

Of course, something is bound to interfere with what you want to do—if you let it. Nearly everyone is hypnotized by the false belief that they are "too busy" or that there is "not enough time" to do the one really important thing they want to do. This is nonsense. Just get what you must do clearly in mind, and do it. It is as simple as that. I know, because I have learned it the hard way.

Then, too, we often do not know we can do a thing *until we do it.* Doing it convinces us that we can. You will be surprised how easy a thing becomes when you learn how to do it. Many times it is simply a matter of "act as though you were, *and you will be.*"

Here are three bad habits that block effective action.

1. Contemplation of work to be done
2. False belief in difficulty
3. Procrastination

Meet each task as it presents itself. Don't just sit there and look at work, thinking of how much you have to do. Do the first thing that needs to be done and you will be on your way. "Start a journey of a thousand miles by taking the first step."

During his efforts to find a substance to use as a filament for the incandescent lamp, Thomas A. Edison's assistants reported failure after 965 attempts.

"It simply cannot be done," they stated.

"Get back to the laboratory," commanded the great inventor.

"You've just discovered 965 ways that are wrong. Now find me the right one."

They found the right filament during the next few experiments and the incandescent lamp has changed our lives. What if Edison had given up? How many times have *you* given up too quickly? It is never a matter of a thing being difficult or impossible to do. It is just that we don't know how at that particular point. Learn how; then do it.

I was once telling Dr. Ernest Holmes of some things I wanted to change in my life and of the difficulty which I was having in bringing about those changes. He stated the principle very clearly: "You are starting on the wrong end. Don't try to make anything happen. Just change yourself inside, and you will spend the rest of your life carrying out the changes which you have effected there. What you do will be right when you get right within yourself."

Every action is an expression of what we are. Prepare yourself as a person and then express yourself intelligently, purposefully and with love. As Kahlil Gibran rightly said, "Work is love made visible."

Decide what you are going to do, then:

> Do it well;
> Do it thoroughly;
> Do it now.

Be sure, however, that what you have to do is important. Take a personal inventory of yourself and then get out and get going. Follow these three steps:

1. Get an idea.
2. Develop it in treatment and prayer.
3. Carry it out. (Remember: do not depart from your inner discipline because of possible outer confusion.)

When you make up your mind to do something, don't just *talk* about it. *Do* something about it. You may say, "But I don't feel like it." Nonsense! That is part of the job! See that you *do* feel like it;

that's where your inner work in treatment and prayer comes in. If you wait until you feel like it, you may *never* feel like it. Start on a project and you release a power dynamic which will carry you along to completion.

Jesus gave us three action steps to help us get started:

1. "Ask and it shall be given you."
2. "Seek and ye shall find."
3. "Knock and it shall be opened unto you."

We must take the initiative. Everything else in the creative process follows automatically.

Prepare yourself for action as follows:

1. Sit down. Relax. Stop thinking of all the things you need to do.
2. Refresh your mind by thinking about something pleasant.
3. Plan one definite thing you want to do and treat upon it.
4. Go out and start to work on it. Keep at it and something will happen.

Here is another sequence to follow which will help you do the job:

1. Give thanks for all the good in your life.
2. Recognize the presence and help of a Superior Power.
3. Whatever you have to do—*know* that you can do it.
4. Do it. Act confidently.

Happy hunting!

DAILY GUIDE TO ACTION

Today I go forward into life, doing what needs to be done to the best of my ability. I let no grass grow under my feet. I am vigorous and strong, filled with vitality and energy, and the desire to do all good things. Nothing stands in the way of my full and complete expression. I know that no one can do for me that which I need to do for myself. I have my row to hoe, so I hoe it. I have my mountain to climb, and I climb it. I arise, take up my bed and walk into my house. I am in the swing of things today.

Lethargy, procrastination and inaction are things of the past. I know who I am and where I am going. I am on my way. I "lift that bale," I "tote that barge." I thrill to the dynamic force which is surging through my entire being. I act from the tremendous potential within me. I have a powerful head of steam, and I use it to turn the wheels of the magnificent machinery which God has given me.

I go where I need to go; I do what I need to do. I wait for no one, nor do I depend upon any outer thing to get me started. I am my own self-starter. I get on with this business of living now. Joyously I embrace every task. Eagerly I move ahead to claim what life has in store for me. Vigorously I cut through all difficulties. I know that with God all things are possible, so why should I worry? Nothing stands in my way. I do what needs to be done, and I do it with a happy heart. I do each job with gusto and enthusiasm. I am in tune with life, and the free, full flow of spiritual energy is surging through me now.

I am on my way. I get out and get going today. And so it is.

13

❖ ❖ ❖

How to Build a Better Life

"Never mind, Carl," my mother said soothingly as she put her arm around my father's bent shoulders. "We'll try again next year."

Slowly my little brother and I followed our parents back to the farmhouse through the parched fields of wheat which had been so green and had held so much promise of abundance just a few hours before. It was stiflingly hot.

A week before, the wind and the rain had robbed us of part of our wheat crop. That wasn't so bad. Even though it entailed considerable loss in potential harvest, the flattened wheat could be used for hay. We still had a good stand of wheat left. But now, with the heat, we were losing that, too, in our never-ending battle with the elements.

The heat had come with terrifying suddenness that late June day—about three weeks too soon. The tender green wheat plants were not yet ready to ripen, and the soft milk in the heads hardened and dried before the kernels were fully formed. The leaves curled pitifully, and the stalks of grain which had stood so straight and brave a few hours before, now drooped defeatedly across the hundreds of acres of rolling hills of our wheat farm.

It was a bitter blow; another crop failure. We had lost out in this and other ways for three years in a row.

"What's the use, Jo?" my father said dejectedly to my mother as he surveyed his ruined crop. "I don't see how we're going to make it through another year."

"We'll find a way, Carl. We'll make it, and then we'll try again next year. All we need is one good crop to solve all our problems."

The courageous ring in my mother's voice was a shot in the arm to all of us. Somehow we knew that everything was going to be all right.

And it was. Even though the wheat crop that year was a failure, my father was able to salvage enough of the harvest to make a payment on his bills, loans, and mortgages and get his credit extended for another year—until next season's harvest.

Many farmers went broke and lost their farms that year, but my father pulled through. Somehow or another our family always managed to.

"We have to make it." I clearly recall my father's often-repeated affirmation of more than thirty years ago. "Where would I go if I gave up now?"

"We will make it, Carl—together—all of us. We'll all help." My mother's quiet statements of faith always strengthened us.

It adds up to a matter of cooperation with life rather than resistance to it. Cooperation is an attitude of mind—the final and completing one of the twelve steps on the Ladder of Accomplishment which we have been developing in this book.

Cooperation is our final step because it utilizes all the other basic attitudes, fusing them together into a circle of completion. Life cooperates with us as we cooperate with life. All we have to do is to learn how. A consistent attitude of cooperation brings accomplishment in releasing and expressing the magnificent potential within each one of us. As we keep eternally at it, cooperating with the tremendous forces at our disposal, we cannot help but fulfill our purpose and destiny. We just need to understand how to do it, and then do it. Victory comes to those who refuse to give up.

We determine our own fate in life. Accept this principle, dedicate yourself to purpose, develop a workable philosophy of life based upon the ideas which we have been discussing in this book, and determine to make something of your life. You are the only person in the world who can do it.

"God grant me the serenity to accept the things I cannot change, courage to change the things I can, and wisdom to know the difference," states Reinhold Niebuhr's great prayer, which has been adopted by Alcoholics Anonymous.

This prayer, together with the famous "twelve steps," has helped hundreds of thousands of alcoholics face themselves and adjust to purposeful living. When alcoholics stop fighting themselves and life and admit that they simply cannot drink, they find an inner peace and strength which helps them get straightened out. When you and I learn how to cooperate with life instead of resisting it, we will be able to do the same thing.

Learn to Cooperate with Life

Think of yourself as rowing a boat in the great Stream of Life whose mighty current moves us along to our destination of fulfillment. If we move with the current, life is easy and pleasant. If we insist upon rowing against it, we wear ourselves out to no avail, miss the fun of life, and finally lose out on its rich rewards.

Learn to understand the laws of life and to cooperate with them. The forces of nature are waiting to be harnessed and used. Life flows through us automatically when we stop resisting it with negative mental and emotional attitudes. By this time, as you have begun to apply the techniques of this book toward building the twelve basic constructive attitudes, you will find that things are becoming easier for you and you are getting greater results. Success is inevitable when we learn how to cooperate with life. Success is largely a matter of being at peace within yourself. Peace of mind comes when we learn the principle of cooperation.

When my mother and father were faced with the long, cold, hungry winter after the crop failure, they spent no time crying over spilt milk. They were faced with a problem and they did something about it. A solution soon presented itself. My mother had always made excellent butter and cottage cheese for our own use. Whenever anyone came to our house for dinner they would express the wish that they could serve these products in their own homes. Mother remembered these compliments and it gave her an idea—she would see that they got their wish. Our family went into the cottage cheese and butter business. As soon as the word got around, we were swamped with customers. We all pitched in and helped to make butter and cottage cheese in the kitchen of our farm home. Then my father and my brother and I delivered the delicious products to our many customers in town a few miles away.

Our home industry brought us through the winter with flying colors. This little incident is a perfect example of how to cooperate with a situation instead of resisting it. Life is a matter of teamwork—of cooperation with ourselves and the forces within us, with God, and with other people.

Prayer treatment is for the purpose of aligning ourselves with the creative power of mind and cooperating with it. The final step of prayer is one of release and acceptance. Since Chapter 7 we have been dealing with thought, feeling and action as the phases of the creative process which lead up to the final step of acceptance. In this final step we say, "Release your treatment. Give thanks and let it happen." Now is the time to let go and cooperate with the creative process as it unfolds, and let the good which you have had in mind take place in your experience.

Cooperation is a way of life. The successful person is the one who has learned to live effortlessly, who is able to adjust to every situation and make the best and the most of it. We are cooperating with life when we:

1. Learn how to forgive.
2. Learn how to pray.
3. Learn how to give.
4. Learn how to receive.
5. Learn how to adjust.

How to Overcome Resistance

Each of these valuable lessons of life helps to remove the inner conflicts which cause resistance. Resistance produces fatigue, and fatigue robs us of efficiency, health and balance. Many people are chronically tired because they do not like the work they are doing, or because they are not intelligent in their planning and organizing. Thus a feeling of overload develops in their lives.

The proper attitude toward our work and responsibilities is essential. We do not become tired from our actual work nearly as much as from our negative attitudes of resistance toward it. Our inner anxieties and pressure drives wear us out, but intelligently directed work should be more of a refilling process than a depleting one. Work can actually produce the energy to do more work. Action generates action. We can actually become refreshed by the most intensive effort when we enjoy what we are doing and learn how to utilize and cooperate with powers within us.

Jesus said, "I of myself do nothing. The Father that dwelleth within me, He doeth the works." Jesus had learned completely the lesson of cooperation. The "father" which He refers to here is the subconscious mind, which He had conditioned to cooperate with the universal subjective mind—the creative power of God indwelling. The life of Jesus provides a model for us to follow in learning how to cooperate with and get the most out of life. He was able to achieve the results He did by:

1. Seeking nothing
2. Giving everything
3. Loving all people
4. Trusting God
5. Living each moment fully

The life of Jesus and the lives of all great men illustrate the results which can be achieved when we learn how to overcome resistance with cooperation.

Of course, we are bound to have problems and difficult situations in life. It is through them that we grow. When we learn to look for the lesson instead of fighting the problem, we will always find the help, the courage and the strength which is needed to move us on to victory and greater accomplishment. Struggle and resistance can only hold us back. Remember, you will never be free *from* a situation until you become free *in* it.

We become free when we learn how to cooperate with life. This entails an understanding of ourselves, and faith in a power which is greater than we are. Life can be a pretty hopeless proposal unless we have faith. And faith itself is cooperation.

Healing Through Cooperation

Healing comes about when resistance is removed and our attitudes of mind cooperate with the free, full flow of the inner perfection.

"Will you treat for our grandchild?" an elderly couple once beseeched my wife and me in Philadelphia. "He is only two years old but he has an ugly skin condition on his back: the doctors say it is incurable. There must be some help for him. We just can't bear to think of him growing up with this affliction."

"There is no need for him to," I comforted them. "Please tell us about it."

It seemed that the child's back had broken out in ugly running sores a few weeks after birth, and no remedy had helped. The child was in constant pain, and cried incessantly.

We asked some questions about the parents. We explained that conditions in young children are invariably the result of a negative and destructive emotional environment caused by the attitudes and feelings of the parents. We asked to talk to them. Against his will, the father, a tense and defensive young man in his early twenties, came to see us. After we had gained his confidence and explained our work, he told us his story.

He was frightened, and he resented the child. Having married very young, he was unprepared for the responsibilities of married life. But although the young couple had difficulties from the very beginning, their love had kept them together. However, when the baby arrived, the father, already worried and chafing under his responsibilities, treated him as an intruder and would have nothing to do with him. This naturally hurt the young mother, and the home life became miserable for everyone, including the new baby, who soon developed the "incurable" skin condition.

Defensive though the father was, he could readily see the connection between his behavior and his child's condition. He wanted to change, and asked us to help him. We started by helping him to get rid of his fear of responsibility. When the fear started to leave him, his defensive attitude lessened, and his resentment toward the child turned to love. Our explanation and discussion was followed by periods of prayer treatment, during which the young man came to realize what a wonderful thing it was to be married and to have a family.

This treatment released the natural love that the father had for his child, which had been misdirected because of immaturity and fear. Remember, we were asked to treat the child; but since the child's condition merely represented the effect of wrong emotional attitudes in the parents, we treated the father, in whom the real cause lay.

Immediate results were achieved. The child's condition soon started to clear up; within two weeks it had completely disappeared. We only saw the young father twice, and we never did see the baby. We didn't need to. We were working with Principle, and it always knows what to do on the individual level when we cooperate with it.

Healing results when we cooperate with the natural inner flow of perfection and right action. "To heal" means "to make whole." We become "whole" or "healed" when every part of our being cooperates with the natural order of things. Spiritual mind healing, the basis of our work, is a matter of removing the mental and emotional blocks—the false beliefs and negative conditionings—which keep us from this cooperation. The job is done by conditioning the mind along the lines of our twelve basic attitudes. A healthy mind automatically produces a healthy baby and harmonious conditions on every level. And cooperation is one of the prerequisites.

"You will never have normal vision," the doctor decreed. "But an operation will save your sight. We'll operate on the right eye now and the left one within a few months, when I return to the city."

This was a bitter verdict for the middle-aged artist. She had called my wife to her bedside at the hospital on the eve of the operation, which she hoped would correct the eye condition that was threatening her career.

Bernice's treatment work was directed toward relaxation and a release of tension and worry. The patient's mind was conditioned into an attitude of complete cooperation with the doctor and the operation, but it was also pointed out that the success of the operation also depended upon cooperation with the natural healing action that is constantly taking place within the body when we let it.

The operation was successful and the eye surgeon left for an extended European tour.

"By the time I return, this eye will have healed and then we'll operate on the other one," was his parting remark.

"I don't want to have that other operation," the woman later told Bernice. "There must be another way."

"There is," Bernice affirmed. "The important thing is—do you believe it?"

"I think so," was the reply. "Help me to. I will do anything you say."

Receiving this promise of cooperation, my wife worked with the artist in treatment every day for several months. Results were amazing.

The eye healed with such rapidity that the woman was released from the hospital much earlier than had been expected. She became a serious student of the Science of Mind and determined to cooperate with the healing treatment in every way.

"But remember," Bernice pointed out, "we are also cooperating with the doctors in every way. The results we achieve must check out medically. The doctors are instruments of God also."

She was pointing out the scientific basis of our work—the principle of cooperation and common sense that makes it so effective. Our approach is not opposed to the medical profession. We believe that the needs of the individual must be met at every level. Spiritual mind therapy provides the coordinating factor that brings the whole picture together. The individual's needs must be met at the level of his understanding. Constant growth at the spiritual level increases the understanding. When this is under way, lesser means are unnecessary.

Bernice and her patient worked toward the major objective of the restoration of perfect sight. This entailed two definite steps:

1. Complete healing and restoration of perfect vision to the eye that had been operated upon.

2. Healing of the other eye so that an operation would not be necessary.

They were successful on both counts. The doctor was amazed upon his return to find that not only had the eye that had been operated upon healed so perfectly that there was no "blind-spot," which ordinarily persists in such cases, but that the other eye had cleared to such a degree that surgery was unnecessary. When he learned what was being done he gave it his complete blessing and cooperated in every way.

The patient's improvement was constant. Her vision became so much better over a period of time that she was able to discard her thick glasses, and eventually passed the eye test for her driver's license without them.

Treatment continued for a period of several years, during which the artist cooperated completely and applied herself diligently to the process of reconditioning her subconscious mind. She had a great deal at stake. She got great results. You can do the same if you are willing to apply yourself with equal diligence and cooperation.

Life cooperates with us when we cooperate with life. The champion in any sporting event learns how to harness his strength and energy so that his efforts produce maximum results. He learns how to overcome resistance outside and inside himself so that nothing will stand in the way of his achievement. Previously unbeaten records topple every day. The 4-minute mile was once but a mythical possibility. Once the mark was broken, however, the barrier was removed from athlete's minds, and now any number of runners have run the mile under 4 minutes. The same principle applies to the pole vault, the shot-put, and many other athletic events.

Once something is achieved, the false belief in its impossibility is removed from our minds and we go ahead and do what we have to do without being hampered by the resistance of negative attitudes of fear and doubt. As Krishnamurti says, "What man has done, man can do. I am man but also God in man; I can do this thing and I will." Repeat this statement to yourself until you believe it completely. All resistance is dissolved as you release the magnificent potential within you. Believe in yourself. Focus your mind upon what you can do, and do it. The mighty forces of the universe will cooperate with you when you give them a chance.

Take an inventory of whatever situation confronts you and approach it as follows:

If it takes planning—plan it.
If it takes work—do it.
If it takes money—use it.
If it takes cooperation—give it.

A giving attitude toward life is an affirmation of faith and cooperation. When we learn how to give, we are using the principle of release, which removes resistance and limitation and makes it possible for us to receive the maximum. Practice these principles of generosity:

Give of yourself.
Give of your interest.
Give of your services.
Give of your material substance.

Be sensible in all that you do, but cultivate an attitude of willingness to do whatever is necessary and right. Go all the way with life and life will go all the way with you. Cooperate with life by constantly endeavoring to make the most of yourself. Great rewards come to those who cooperate with the forces of the universe.

Now let us examine these four characteristics which are aspects of the cooperative attitude: humor, humility, generosity, and dependability.

Humor

"Laugh and the world laughs with you; weep and you weep alone." The world just doesn't have much use for a sourpuss. Take your work seriously, but never yourself. Learn to look at the lighter side of things. Be pleasant in all situations. Have a good time in everything you do. There is little point to life unless we enjoy it.

When we align ourselves with the lighter side of things we are buoyed up by a power which lifts our burdens, lightens our load, and makes life a free and glorious adventure.

Humility

A humble, simple attitude of gratitude and expectancy is essential for true cooperation with life. Attitudes of self-importance and self-aggrandizement only get in the way. "Blessed are the meek: for they shall inherit the earth," states one of the great Beatitudes. Modesty is evidence of inner peace and strength. A humble person understands his true place in the great scheme of things. All truly great people are humble, and live in awe of the magnificence within and around them. Jesus said, "The words that I speak unto you I speak not of myself: but the Father that dwelleth in me, He doeth the works."

Generosity

Generosity is love in action. Cultivate a warm, outgoing personality. Look for ways to give of yourself. Participate in the great unfoldment of life. Hold nothing back. Live each moment fully. Give everyone the benefit of the doubt. Recognize that everyone is doing the best that they can at their particular level of understanding. Keep criticism and judgment to yourself, and be ever free to offer encouragement and approbation.

We have been given the great gift of life to use as we see fit. Express it generously. Give of your strength and abilities wherever they are needed. Give yourself away and you will find your own soul.

Dependability

We cherish nothing quite so much as a friend whom we can depend upon. Someone has said, "A friend is someone who knows all about you and loves you anyway."

A dependable person is a pillar of strength toward which people are drawn and to which all good things come. A sense of duty, willingness and responsibility is a major prerequisite for cooperating with life. Be steady, strong and capable and the riches of the kingdom will come to you. Be honest with yourself; be the kind of person that others can trust; carry your share of the load and carry it well. Cooperate in this way and the entire universe will cooperate with you. Do a good job upon yourself and everything else will take care of itself.

Develop your cooperation in four main categories:

1. Cooperate with life.
2. Cooperate with time.
3. Cooperate with yourself.
4. Cooperate with others.

Cooperate with Life

Life is for living. Flow with the tide. Use the natural current of life rather than resisting it. Look for the best in everything and everybody. Develop the twelve basic affirmative attitudes of this book. Develop yourself as a whole person. Develop inner balance. Use your magnificent inner potential.

Cooperate with Time

You have all the time there is. There is time to do whatever needs to be done if we plan and organize efficiently. Outer hurry is evidence of inner stress. There is a time for action and a time for release and reflection. Don't try to fill every moment. Make time your friend and ally. It will cooperate with you and lengthen the days of your life.

Cooperate with Yourself

We never really resist or fight anything but ourselves. You are your own best friend. Get on good terms with yourself. Establish harmony with the inhabitants of your own household. "The kingdom of God is within you." Establish residence there. Your power comes from perfect agreement between your will and your imagination. See that your thoughts, feelings and actions are perfect allies.

Cooperate with Others

An ability to get along with other people must be developed and sustained. No one can go it alone. We need each other. We are our brother's keeper. Life is a matter of helping each other. Happiness and good fortune belong to us. "Do unto others as you would have others do unto you." The good that you do for others you are doing for yourself.

THE SPIRITUAL HELICOPTER

Perspective is essential to the development of true cooperation. We remove the resistance which comes from too much involvement with details by learning to see things in their true perspective. We establish perspective and see the various aspects of life in their true relationship to the whole when we learn how to raise our own consciousness. This is done through the development of the twelve basic affirmative attitudes to which we have devoted this book.

Obviously, our job is to rise above human problems and identify ourselves with the Infinite Power if we are to experience life's true potential.

The "spiritual helicopter" is one technique for accomplishing our goal of dissolving resistance and releasing our natural capacities into the flow of full cooperation with life.

When confronted with problems and difficulties, simply rise above them. Visualize how a helicopter rises straight up from the ground. You do the same thing. Get into your helicopter (your own mind-consciousness), start your motor (your inner capacity for accomplishment), start the blades of the propeller (your ideas and attitudes) rotating, and let the resulting power lift you up to a higher point of view. Try it right now. Life's battles are not won in the trenches of travail and resistance. They are won in the air of higher consciousness. Use your spiritual helicopter to lift you up into an attitude of release and cooperation, where difficulty and resistance disappear and higher currents of life freely circulate.

Use these ten steps to develop cooperation with life:

1. Learn to say, "It doesn't matter just because it doesn't matter."
2. Take care of the big things and the little things will take care of themselves.
3. Never worry about anything that can be taken care of with money.
4. Don't worry about the other person or what he is going to do. You be responsible for you.
5. If you have something to do, don't fight it; do it.
6. Enjoy everything you do. Look forward to everything in life as a joyous experience.
7. Stop being concerned about what other people think about you. Watch what you are thinking about other people.
8. Plan intelligently and follow through.
9. Don't ask, "What's in this for me?" but ask, "Is this a good thing for me to do?"
10. Use life; don't abuse it.

Daily Guide to Cooperation

Today I cooperate with life and life cooperates with me. I am a member of the team and I give it everything I have. I hold nothing back. I give of myself completely as I get into the swing of things and move steadily along to victory and accomplishment. All resistance is removed as I follow a course of full and consistent cooperation.

I learn to "let go and let God." I release all concern over situations and things. I rise above the petty attitudes which have held me down. All selfishness and conceit are removed from my consciousness. I become a bigger and better person as I cooperate with larger goals and purposes. I am interested only in the greater good. I cooperate with everyone and everything that helps to make this world a better place.

I cooperate with life. I flow with it. I live it abundantly. I develop my inner vision and I go where my vision takes me. "I will lift up mine eyes until the hills, from whence cometh my help." I rise above the trivial and commonplace. I use the natural power which God has given me to accomplish all good things in my world.

I cooperate with other people. I offer myself to the service of God and all mankind. I am a team player. I do everything that is necessary to help bring about that which is for the greatest good of the greatest number. I love people and I will do anything for them. I hold nothing back. I have been given all things, and I give everything in return. I cooperate fully in bringing about all good and noble things.

I cooperate with God and myself by giving my magnificent potential full expression at all times. I say, "God, use me." I go joyously forward into life. I offer my complete cooperation in helping to establish the kingdom of heaven on earth. I am a cooperative person now. And so it is.

14

❖ ❖ ❖

Life Is a Daily Proposition

Life is exactly what we make it. It is up to us. Our attitudes toward our days and toward our lives as a whole determine the results which we achieve.

Throughout this book we have stressed the importance of developing the twelve basic constructive mental and emotional attitudes which will insure success and victory in this business of living. As you practice the techniques which have been suggested, and as you develop the constructive approach through the use of the Daily Guides, you will move surely and steadily toward victory and success.

The rewards of life are ours for the taking. But we can't just think and talk about the abundant life. We must do the things which bring it about. Each moment is a precious gift, and what we do with each moment determines the character of the whole sequence of time which makes up our lives. Regular and sustained patterns must be adhered to if we are to realize the fullness of our magnificent potential.

Great artists become great because they work at it through steady application and regular practice. Paderewski, the great pianist, said, "If I miss practicing one day, I know it; if I miss two days, my wife knows it; if I miss a week, everybody knows it." In other words, we cannot keep our "slips" from showing. Every thought, feeling, word and deed plays its part in the final picture of our lives.

In the Lord's Prayer, Jesus stressed the importance of living one day at a time when He prayed, "Give us this day our daily bread," and in the Sermon on the Mount when He instructed, "Sufficient unto the day is the evil thereof," indicating that if we meet our problems and challenges as they arise we are doing all that can be expected of us. But we must take care of each moment as we live it. It is when we let things pile up that we get into difficulty. The old adage, "Never put off until tomorrow what you can do today" is still a most reliable guide.

In Alcoholics Anonymous the members are urged to practice sobriety one day at a time. Anything repeated over and over forms a habit. Daily repetition of constructive attitudes and actions soon forms a solid structure of constructive living.

"Every day in every way I'm getting better and better" was Emile Coué's simple affirmation which helped millions form affirmative patterns of thought. Of course, there is more to building a constructive life than just repeating catch-phrase affirmations, but the affirmative attitude is the first step toward releasing your magnificent potential. Everything starts with thought. Thoughts are responded to by feeling. This builds attitudes. The prevailing mental and emotional attitudes determine experience. Experiences form the pattern of our lives.

In the same way, seconds accumulate into minutes, and the sequence unfolds through hours, days, weeks, months and years to form the span of our lifetime. Eternity is being expressed through each of us right now—in this moment. Live it fully and well. Give it the best that you have, and the results will take care of themselves.

It is the attitude that is the important thing. How do you start your day? Do you awaken joyously and say, "Thank you, God—another day!" Or do you drag out of bed groaning, "Oh God! Another day." There isn't very far you can go with the latter attitude, but there is no limit to what your day can bring you if you sustain the first attitude of thankfulness and enthusiasm.

Awaken with the statement, "I don't know what's ahead for me today, but I know it can only be good," then go ahead and live the day so that this becomes true. Sustain the realization, "Today I am one step closer to my demonstration of complete good." Start each day afresh in this way, and live each moment as if it were both your first and your last. Watch children. See how interested and curious they are! Each moment holds the promise of glorious adventure. They can't wait to see what happens next. They live with their total being. They give their entire attention to what they are doing, pursue it to its conclusion, then go on to something else, repeating the process. As we do the same we will constantly grow into ever greater accomplishment.

Live in the here and the now. Make each moment a masterpiece of living. Life is an upward spiral. Get into the swing of it. The whole is made up of the sum total of *all* the parts. Live each moment so that it can be taken as an example for all people to follow. Life is a series of highs and lows. Anyone can handle the high points. The big moments take care of themselves. It is the valleys and the plateaus that we must learn to handle.

Life is a daily proposition but it doesn't have to be a struggle. However, it *will* be a struggle if we approach it as one. Attitudes of fear, hate, inferiority, guilt, conflict, rejection and anxiety produce all kinds of difficulties. But by the same token, attitudes of faith, love, confidence, understanding, cooperation, acceptance and peace make life a glorious adventure. Joy, fulfillment and accomplishment come to us when we establish and sustain constructive inner attitudes.

Life stretches endlessly before us, but don't think of how far you have to go; think of how far you have come. Make each day a masterpiece. First, establish inner order and direction by using the "Golden Bridge," which we developed in Chapter 11. Constructively rehearse the span of each day and follow it as best you can. Affirm daily: "The Power that created me and put me here motivates and activates me throughout this day." Use this as an anchor whenever things go wrong, then go back over the Golden Bridge each night before retiring, correcting your mistakes and clarifying the inner pattern of right action. In this way, each day becomes a clear-cut unit in the structure of your life.

Go back over this book, studying each chapter carefully until you have a clear understanding of each of the twelve basic steps. Make each one an important tool to use in building your life. Condition your mind with these constructive attitudes so that they will be your automatic reactions in all situations.

Go over all twelve points several times each day and use them to prepare for every situation which confronts you. If things go wrong, or if you are not getting the desired results, find out in which of the points you are weak; then make a special effort to strengthen them. As you follow this procedure you will steadily become more balanced, well-rounded, and effectual. There is no substitute for steady, sustained spiritual development. Mastery of each of the twelve steps on the Ladder of Accomplishment will give you just that. Live them daily and you will be rewarded by results which will prove that you are recognizing, believing in, and using your magnificent potential.

Take time right now to review the twelve steps in your mind:

1. Relaxation
2. Expectation
3. Recognition
4. Unification
5. Dedication
6. Intention
7. Identification
8. Conviction
9. Realization
10. Projection
11. Action
12. Cooperation

Together they form the complete prayer. Prayer is a way of life. You now have the tools for effective prayer—the key which releases your magnificent potential.

You *are* magnificent. Know it. Live from this premise, and "surely, goodness and mercy shall follow *you* all the days of *your* life, and *you* will dwell in the house of the Lord forever."

Good luck and God bless you.

MASTER GUIDE TO DAILY LIVING

My house is in order at all times. I live from the center of complete balance and integration. I am whole in spirit, mind and body. I recognize my magnificent inner potential and express it in all that I do. I build the Ladder of Accomplishment within my mind and heart. It is the structure upon which I weave the perfect pattern of my life.

Relaxation

Life is in free, full flow through me now. I relax and enjoy it. All strain, pressure and tension are dissolved from me as I learn to "let go and let God." I reside in the peace and quiet of an all-powerful inner strength. I am reposed but ready at all times. I am relaxed in mind and body. I know that "easy does it," and I do all things easily now.

Expectation

I expect the best to come to me and it always does. I experience right action in everything I do because I always expect it. I look forward to each moment as a tremendous new experience. I anticipate a steadily unfolding progression of good in my life. I am an incurable optimist. I have great expectations and I know that every one of them is an already accomplished fact.

Recognition

Everywhere I look, the Infinite lies stretched in smiling repose. Life reveals its secrets to me as I recognize the truth that lies at the center of all things. Everything has meaning, and my life is devoted to discovering this meaning. I recognize the Ultimate Reality which is God. I recognize that I am an individualized expression of this One First Cause. I recognize the wonder and beauty of life today.

Unification

I am one with all that is. Everything that is, is part of me. I am unified in spirit, mind and body. I am a whole person now. My completeness is evidence of my unity with God. I am free from all cross-purposes. I am a complete unit. I am in tune with the Infinite. I am in harmony with the universe. I am part of the One Great Whole, and live accordingly.

Dedication

There is purpose and meaning in everything I do. I am dedicated to noble purpose. I dedicate my life to expressing the magnificence which is God. I dedicate my life to make the most of myself. I dedicate my life to helping other people. I dedicate my life to making the world a better place in which to live. I dedicate myself to making a good job of this business of living.

Intention

I intend to succeed and I do. I intend to be happy and I am. I intend to be healthy all the days of my life. I experience perfect health now. I intend to be at my best at all times. I intend to accomplish many wonderful things, and I am busy working on them. I intend to discover the secret of eternal life by making everything I do a contribution to my growth and to the betterment of all people.

Identification

I marry my ideal. I am completely identified with everything constructive and good. My mind adopts the attitude that my every prayer is answered and my every dream is already true. I am permanently identified with the Infinite Mind which makes this true. I am identified with the larger picture. I am a big person. I am permanently identified with all good things.

Conviction

All doubt is removed from my mind. I have a strong and vital faith. Perfect love casts out all fear. I have a conviction of inner wholeness. I have a conviction of purposeful right action. I have a conviction of the constant availability of God at all times. I have a conviction of immortality and eternalness. I am convinced that "God's in his heaven and all's right with the world"—now and always.

Realization

Today I experience the perfect peace which comes from the realization that all good things which I desire are already true. I just need to accept them. I do accept them now. "I and my Father are one." I praise God that good is everywhere. I realize what it means to be a man. I realize the beauty and magnificence of this life which I am privileged to live. I live it fully now.

Projection

What I am goes before me and prepares the way for all that I wish to do. I project the confidence and love which comes from inner security. I think, feel, speak and do only that which is constructive and true. I am quick to praise and encourage others. I work constantly to improve myself. I am a light shining in the darkness. I project a broad, clear beam into my world.

Action

I go purposefully about God's business. I work efficiently and well. There is meaning to all that I do. I never rest on my laurels. I am constantly discovering new ways to be a better person and to do greater things. I carry my load. I gladly accept responsibility. I am a wave in the tide of life, and I am always moving in the right direction. I do joyously all that there is for me to do.

Cooperation

I cooperate with life and life cooperates with me. I can't go it alone, so I don't try. "I can do all things through Christ which strengtheneth me." "I and my Father are one . . . he that hath seen me hath seen the Father." "I do nothing of myself . . . the Father that dwelleth in me, He doeth the works." I cooperate with the laws of life, and "my yoke is easy and my burden is light." I cooperate completely with my Magnificent Potential now and always. And so it is.

INDEX

About the Author

DONALD CURTIS, a leading teacher and writer in the field of New Thought for more than forty years, is recognized as a foremost authority in personal spiritual development. Ordained by Dr. Ernest Holmes, founder of Science of Mind, Dr, Curtis has ministered to large congregations in New York, Los Angeles, and Dallas, has lectured throughout the world, and has been honored with a Lifetime Achievement Award from Founders Church of Religious Science. A former actor who has appeared on Broadway and in over two hundred Hollywood films, Dr. Curtis acts as a guide for his many students as they enter higher levels of awareness and embark upon a path which leads to richer, fuller living.

A full listing of Dr. Curtis's books, lessons, and study material will be sent upon request. You may also receive information regarding his speaking engagements and workshops schedules.

For information or to arrange lectures and seminars with Dr. Curtis, contact:

Golden Bridge Literary Agency
Karen Lee Curtis, Authors' Representative
65910 Fourteenth Street
Desert Hot Springs, CA 92240
1-800-429-2794
Fax: 1-619-329-8444